Guiding Light

Reflect on the Word

CYCLE B

Homilies by Fr. Joe Robinson

Shepherds of Christ Publications
P.O. Box 627
China, Indiana 47250 USA

Toll free USA: (888) 211-3041
Tel: (812) 273-8405
Fax: (812) 273-3182
Email: info@sofc.org
http://www.sofc.org

ISBN: 978-1-934222-30-0

Second Printing: 2012

In honor
of our
Beloved Priests

Table of Contents
Cycle B - 2011

Foreward

For years all of us have gone to St. Boniface Church in Cincinnati, Ohio. Our family first lived in this parish – Some of the streets named after our relatives –

Fr. Carter was the founder of the Shepherds of Christ Movement and I, Rita Ring, co-founder –

But my brother, Fr. Joseph Robinson was an important part of my life and our lives as we went to his most holy Masses and listened to his homilies as we formed more and more as a body of people producing the Priestly Newsletter and beginning prayer chapters.

God blessed me and all of us being able to go to his Masses and listen to his homilies –

It is a tremendous honor Fr. Joe has allowed us to share these great gifts with you – for greater holiness and knowing more and more about God –

This is the fifth in a series of these homily books – dedicated to our priests, out of love for our beloved Church and all the souls of the world.

As you use these great teachings of homilies Sunday after Sunday – please pray the prayers with us as a network of prayer – praying for the priests, the Church and the world –

I thank God every day for the gift of my older brother who has been an important instrument in his priesthood in my life and the lives of all who went to St. Boniface for Mass.

Rita Robinson Ring

Co-founder, Shepherds of Christ Movement

Certificate of Marriage

I, the undersigned, do hereby certify, that on the 25 day of June A.D. 1936 in the church of St. Boniface I joined in the

Holy Bonds of Matrimony

William M. Robinson and Alice Weber

according to the rites of the Holy Roman Catholic Church.

Witness: Henry J. Robinson
Marie Weber

Rev. John H. Schwartz
Pastor

Dedicated to William and Alice Robinson.

Our Mother and Father married on
June 25, 1936 in St. Boniface Church, Cincinnati.

1st Sunday of Advent
November 30, 2008

INTRODUCTION – (Isaiah 63:16b-17, 19b; 64:2-7) Today's first reading is a desperate prayer for God to come to save his people. It is one of the most sublime prayers we find in Scripture. God's people were suffering; when it was too late they realized they had brought disaster upon themselves because of their pride and failure to listen to God's Word. They ask for his help and forgiveness. It's a good prayer for the beginning of Advent. We ask God to open our hearts to his coming.

HOMILY – (Mark 13:33-37) As we've heard so many times, the word "advent" means "coming." The season of advent is a time to prepare for Christ's coming to us 2000 years ago and Christ's coming to us some day in the future. Jesus tells us emphatically to watch for his coming, to be alert.

In order to watch and to be alert, we have to stay focused, focused on Jesus as our savior and redeemer. Staying focused in this way implies taking time to reflect, to slow down. At the same time our culture is telling us to hurry up, to get our shopping done, our house decorated, our Christmas cards sent, a party here and there to go to. It can really raise a person's anxiety to hear these opposing messages: slow down, hurry up. We are constantly torn in both directions: slow down, hurry up.

There is an insert in today's bulletin giving a few suggestions as to how to think of time and how to manage it. There is an article in the inside page entitled: "A time for Everything" giving some time management ideas that I use most of the time. The only thing is the title is deceptive. You won't get everything done even with the best techniques, so don't plan on it or you'll always be frustrated. You have to put the most important things at the top of your list, so that at least you get those tasks done, while things that are of lesser importance you may never get to. We all have only 24 hours to work with and there is no trick to turning 24 hours into any more. Prioritize is the key idea. You might find the article helpful especially at this time of the year.

In today's gospel Jesus is telling us about prioritizing. He's going to return and we don't know when. We must be watchful - that means keeping ourselves ready for him to return - which means keeping our busy lives in perspective. One practical way to do that is to take time to meditate. There are myriad ways to meditate such as: 1) to have a conversation with God or with Jesus, 2) to prayerfully read the Scriptures, 3) to look over the day and ask yourself what went well and what you are grateful for and what didn't and why, 4) to quiet our mind and say nothing, just giving God a chance to possibly say something to us or 5) to say the rosary. Whatever way you choose, it will help you stay more peaceful, reduce stress, lower you blood pressure and help you stay focused as to what's important in life and what is not so important.

I want to assure you I enjoy all the nice things about Christmas, all the lights and decorations, the celebrations, the gatherings with friends and family. After all, the birth of our king and savior is worthy of a grand celebration. But his birth is just the first step in the process of his coming. He comes with light and grace and love and peace to us now when we come to him in faith and prayer. And he will come again to take us to himself "so that where I am, you also may be." Since we don't know when he's going to come for us, we must be always ready for him to come knocking on our door to tell us he is ready for us. That's important.

With all the stuff that happens at this time of the year and the stuff we feel we must have ready for Christmas, we cannot forget that the child whose birth we celebrate was born in poverty, lived in poverty, died in poverty and taught us not to make "things" too important in our lives. I'm not a proponent of poverty, but sometimes we forget the meaning of Christmas is not in things but in our hearts.

As we prepare to celebrate Christ's coming in the past, in the present and in the future, we hear him tell us once again "be watchful, be alert."

2nd Sunday of Advent
December 7, 2008

INTRODUCTION – (Isaiah 40:1-5, 9-11; 2 Peter 3: 8-14; Mark 1:1-8) Our first reading today begins a section of Isaiah known as the "Book of Consolation." This section of Isaiah is composed of 15 chapters that were addressed to God's people who for 50 years had been refugees and slaves in Babylon (Iraq today). Isaiah announces God is ready to set them free and bring them back home. The route by which the Lord would lead his people home is referred to as "the way of the Lord." Attention must be given to preparing the way. The route would take them through mountains and desert, a passage most likely through the land that is today Iraq, Syria and Lebanon. The images in today's reading are beautiful, especially the image of God leading his people like a shepherd, but the key idea for today is to prepare the way of the Lord, a theme that John the Baptist takes up 500 years later to call the people of his own day to prepare for the Messiah. The liturgy uses these

Scriptures to call us to prepare not only for Christmas but also for the day when Christ will call us into his eternal kingdom.

HOMILY – I was impressed with the directness and simplicity of how St. Mark begins his gospel. "This is the gospel (the good news) of Jesus Christ, the Son of God." We say it so glibly and so quickly we might miss the importance of these words, so I want to give them some special emphasis. What could be more basic to our faith than our belief that Jesus is not only Messiah and Savior, but that he is Son of God and everything about him is good news for us. That Jesus is Son of God is one of the things that is unique about our faith and different from all other religions. Moses, Mohammed, Buddha, Confucius, whomever, are all revered as prophets who spoke for God or wise and holy people who taught the path to God, but none are honored as God. Jesus is proclaimed in the gospels as God (not "a" God, but "the" God, the only God, one in being with the Father and the Holy Spirit). So Mark gets right to the essence of our faith as he begins his gospel: "This is the good news (the gospel) of Jesus Christ, the Son of God."

Except for two brief references to Mary his mother, St. Mark doesn't spend time telling us anything about Jesus' birth or about his parents. We thank St. Matthew and St. Luke for those beautiful stories which we love to hear again and again about what took place at the time of his birth. In order to stress another concept that is essential for us if we are going to experience the gospel as the good news of Jesus Christ, the Son of God, Mark begins his gospel by telling us about John the Baptist.

It was important for St. Mark to talk about John the Baptist as he began his gospel for two reasons. First of all, many people thought he was the messiah, the savior of God's people. Mark makes it clear in John's own words, "One mightier than I is coming after me. I am not worthy to stoop down and untie his sandals." The second reason it is important to bring up John the Baptist as Mark begins his gospel is the message of the Baptist: prepare.

John the Baptist is not talking about preparing our house, or our gifts, or our meals, or our celebrations, which we always do at this time of year and are delightful traditions. He's talking about preparing our heart. Can we open our hearts to Jesus or to others any more than we already have? Can we say we love God perfectly and completely, our neighbor perfectly and completely? In preparing the way of the Lord, there may not be any mountains or hills of pride that have to come down in our lives. There may not be valleys of spiritual laziness that need to be filled in or rugged land and rough country of serious sin that need to be eliminated to prepare the way for Jesus' coming. But if we think hard, we might discover little spots here and there where we could love God or others more. "Prepare the way of the Lord" was the message of the Baptist and the message of the gospels. We do not enter into God's kingdom by accident or by default. It's like anything else in life, if we want something worthwhile or to accomplish anything worth accomplishing, we need to prepare. Many people assume God's kingdom will be somehow different than everything else in life, that it will take little or no effort on our part to be part of it, that somehow it will come to everyone automatically. The gospels do not tell us that. With St. Mark and with John the Baptist they tell us quite simply and directly: Prepare!

Feast of the Immaculate Conception
December 8, 2009

HOMILY – In the first three chapters of the book of Genesis, we hear about the creation of the world and all things in it. The story of creation is not meant to be a documentary that gives us an accurate historical or scientific account. It's not something that was witnessed by CNN and is now being reported on. It is a theology lesson put in story form that tells us as much about God as it does about creation. There are really two stories about creation. The first story puts God's work in the framework of seven days while the second story is more focused on the creation of our first parents and their relationship with God. It was a beautiful, loving and harmonious relationship they had with God until the devil came along disguised as a serpent. The devil was jealous of our first parents and their closeness to God, so the devil talked them into rebelling against God. Thus as St. Paul said: "sin entered into the world," a sin that seems to have become part of our DNA. This is what we call "Original Sin." It's not like some "thing" attached to us, rather it is more like a lack of something, something important is missing, which is the original grace which God blessed us with at the time of creation. This Original Sin is a kind of tendency in all of us to pride, selfishness, self-centeredness. It leads us to rebel against God like our first parents did. We see signs of it everywhere. If we read the whole passage in Genesis, we see that sin affected not only our first parents' relationship with God, but it affected their relationship with each other - they felt shame in the presence of one another. It affected their relationship with the rest of creation - they lost the joy they had in the Garden of Eden and had to struggle with the rest of creation in order to survive. Our first reading does not go into all that. The part of the story that we heard in our first reading has the purpose of pointing out to us that, although we sin, God does not want us to remain in a state of alienation from him. Instead God would rescue the human race from this predicament we find ourselves in. So what we heard in our first reading was an announcement of good news for all of us. God spoke to the serpent, the devil, the evil one and said: "I will put enmity between you and the woman, between your offspring and hers." Enmity: in other words, all our lives we would be struggling with evil. In a poetic way God announces that evil would not win in the struggle. He told the serpent: you might strike at his heel (i.e. you might be able to do some harm to the offspring of the woman) but he will strike at your head (which would imply a fatal blow). The powers of evil will not triumph even though they often seem to. Yet sin is a powerful force, one that humanity is unable to conquer by its own power, its own cleverness, its own politics, its own laws. And so God sent his Son to come to our rescue. God's Son took on our human nature to show us the way back to a loving and harmonious relationship with God. He came to us through a woman whose goodness and holiness was not tainted by this sin that touches all the rest of us. She was full of grace from the very first moment of her existence. God did not think it fitting for the mother of his Son to be touched by sin for she would give birth to the One who would destroy sin and death in us by his own death and resurrection. When Mary was asked if she would be the mother of our Savior and Lord she answered: "May it be done to me according to your word." The answer she gave was the way she lived her whole life: always ready to say "yes" to whatever God asked of her. And so Jesus came to us, he was born, he taught, he healed, he forgave sins, he cast out demons, he died for us. Before he left us to return to the Father he gave us the sacraments to help us overcome sin and to be renewed in God's life. As we honor the Immaculate Virgin Mary, we pray she may inspire us and help us to stay close to God and in his grace by always saying "yes" to God as she did. Amen.

3rd Sunday of Advent

December 14, 2008

INTRODUCTION – (Isaiah 61:1-2a. 10-11; 1 Thessalonians 5:16-24; John 1:6-8, 19-28) As the celebration of Christ's birth draws near, joy is in the air. It's also reflected in today's liturgy - not just in the rose colored vestments but especially in our readings. The prophet in today's first reading is speaking to the people of his own day, a people who had been exiles and slaves in Babylon for 50 years. Their exile was over. They had been set free by the king of Persia who had conquered Babylon. They could go home, rebuild their cities and farms and their Temple. The prophet was rejoicing in what God was doing for his people. This passage encourages us to rejoice in what God is doing for us. Incidentally, in St. Luke's gospel, often called the gospel of joy, this is part of the section from the prophet Isaiah that Jesus chose to read in the synagogue to the people of Nazareth to indicate what his ministry would be about. The response, which is almost always from the Book of Psalms, is today taken from the gospel of Luke. It is Mary's hymn of joy, called the Magnificat, which she enthusiastically proclaimed when she visited her cousin Elizabeth after the annunciation.

HOMILY – We heard God's prophet proclaim great

joy to the Jews that their exile was over. In the response we heard Mary's expression of joy when she visited her cousin Elizabeth. We heard St. Paul in the second reading tell us to rejoice always. I would like to describe each of these with a little more detail, then I have a brief commercial followed by some concluding remarks.

The prophet in today's first reading announced the Babylonian exile was over. Great news! The people, for the most part, were somewhat glad to be set free, but it wasn't an easy time for them. After 50 years they were pretty well settled in Babylon. They had jobs and homes there. Their homes in Israel had been leveled 50 years earlier and there wasn't much to return to. Nothing remained of their beloved Temple, which the Babylonians had destroyed, except a hill covered with rocks and weeds. The prophet had a real challenge encouraging God's people to rejoice in their return home. It was only by having faith in what God was doing for them that they could have joy.

Mary, the mother of Jesus, had every reason to be anxious and depressed. Here she was suddenly going to be a mother. Her husband to be, Joseph, was about to break off the engagement. In just a few months, she would suffer disgrace among her family and friends when it became obvious she was going to have a child without being married. In that society she would have no way to support herself financially without a husband. Yet we hear, as she visits her cousin Elizabeth after the annunciation, how she rejoices, not in her misery, but in what God was about to do.

As we know from Paul's writings, his job as a missionary was not an easy one. He tells us in his second letter to the Corinthians that he was beaten numerous times, put in jail, faced angry mobs, had gone without eating or sleeping, faced death, been shipwrecked three times, suffered from cold and pain, and faced dangers from robbers, his own people, even supposed Christians,. Yet he writes to the Thessalonians: "Rejoice always, pray without ceasing, give thanks!" Why? "Because this is the will of God for you." If it is God's will for us that we be joyful, God will certainly help us if we choose to be. Paul is saying we can choose to sit around and feel sorry for ourselves or we can choose to be joyful even in difficult circumstances. We can let self-pity control our lives, or we can choose through faith and with God's help to rejoice. If we can believe in the great things God has done and is about to do for us, we have reason to rejoice.

Let me make a little commercial here. One of the things Paul says is: "give thanks." We certainly do that every time we come to Mass. The very word for the Mass, the Eucharist, means "thanksgiving." There is another way to give thanks today also, through the appeal for the retirement for religious. Most of us were educated by dedicated priests, brothers and sisters who, if they have not died, are now too old to go out and work for a living. There aren't enough younger religious to support them. So they need our help. You can give thanks for what you received years ago by helping them out today. End of commercial.

Even though life is sometimes burdensome and the economy is bad and there are threats all over the world; even though there are a lot of things we can complain about and a lot of things that could be better, we have more reasons to rejoice than any people who ever lived on this planet. We enjoy wonderful physical blessings and our freedom; we have the benefits of modern medicine and conveniences. Yet true joy in our hearts must still go deeper than all the things we have around us for we must rejoice in what God is doing in our life.

St. John the Baptist tells us in today's gospel, "there is one among you whom you do not recognize." This is true. By faith we know he is among us, but if we could really recognize him, we would be so full of joy we would be as if we were in heaven. God's plans for us are grandiose, his light and love so wonderful. If we could experience it all we would be mystics, which wouldn't be all bad. But most of us have to live in faith and hope until God's kingdom is realized in us. So like the people we heard about in today's readings, we rejoice like they did - in faith. Amen.

4th Sunday of Advent

December 21, 2008

INTRODUCTION – (2 Samuel 7:1-5, 8b-12, 14a,16; Luke 1:26-38) Our first reading has to go back to the time when Moses rescued God's people from slavery in Egypt and brought them through the desert to the Promised Land. God made a covenant with his people in the desert. He assured them of his special love and insisted on their total obedience to him. The terms of the covenant (which we usually call the 10 Commandments) were enclosed in a golden box and this box was called the Arc of the Covenant. The top of the Arc had two angels on it and God's invisible throne and presence was envisioned above the angels. This special symbol of God's presence with his people was kept in their midst in a tent for almost 300 years. When King David chose Jerusalem as the center of his kingdom and built his palace there, he decided the Arc should be kept in something more dignified than a tent. He decided to build a house for God, a Temple. That's where today's first reading comes in. God turned down David's proposal but instead said David's son would build the

Temple. However, God said he would build a house for David; i.e., God would establish his kingdom so that one of his descendants would always reign as king. For 400 years, the kings of Judah were of the house of David. Unfortunately, many of the kings led God's people away from God, thus leading the nation to lose its faith and its moral strength. They folded easily when the Assyrians and Babylonians attacked them. The people never forgot God's promise to David and they continued to wait for a king from David's line who would lead them once again. In the gospel, we hear the angel Gabriel announce to Mary she would have a son who would inherit "the throne of David his father, and he would rule over the house of Jacob forever and of this kingdom there would be no end."

HOMILY – The scene in today's gospel takes us 600 years later in history after the last king from David's line had ruled God's people. The Romans were in charge at the time of the gospel and the King in Israel, King Herod the Great, was really a puppet of Rome. But God did not forget his promise to David. The angel Gabriel announces to a young girl, soon to be married to a man named Joseph, who is of the house of David, that she will give birth to a son. Her son will inherit "the throne of David, his father, and he will rule over the house of Jacob forever, and of his kingdom there will be no end." More than a king, the angel announces he will be great and will be called Son of the Most High. His birth would take place in an entirely miraculous way, through the power of the Holy Spirit. From the moment Mary said "yes" to the angel, the Son of God took on our human flesh.

This opens up for me a topic that continues to weigh on me, the miracle of conception in general. Mary's conception of Jesus was indeed unique, through the power of the Holy Spirit, but the conception of each child is something special. A new human being comes into existence at conception. Picture in your imagination, is there any real difference between an infant that is just born and an infant one day from being born? The only difference between the two is where it happens to be living and where it gets its oxygen and nutrition. That's all! Yet the legal systems in so many countries of our world (including our own) make an essential and fundamental distinction between a child just born and one just hours away from being born. They even call them by different names: an infant and a fetus. Legally they say a child just born has all the rights of citizenship, the right to life, liberty and the pursuit of happiness while the other person whose mailing address is still within his or her mother has no rights at all.

A few weeks ago I went to the Freedom Center and I couldn't help but see a parallel between the struggle in our Country over slavery and the struggle over abortion. Slaves were considered to be someone's property, they had no rights, their families could be torn apart, they were not even considered human beings by many people. It took our Country a long time to eliminate slavery and now enlightened countries all over the world recognize slavery as inhuman. No person has the right to treat another as his or her property. Yet, isn't that exactly what's happening with abortion laws. An infant, who is unable to defend itself in any way, is treated as someone's property and can be destroyed at the whim of the owner.

It takes a lot of rationalization to justify that. Yet I recently was in a discussion with a person who should have known better who said, "you don't know whether a fetus is human." I don't know what he thinks it is, a cabbage! If there's life in the mother's womb, there's only one kind of life it can be. I know a doctor who did abortions. He was honest about what he was doing and he didn't whitewash it. He would tell medical students who might be preparing to go into that field that in doing an abortion they are taking human life. I know he suffered a great deal within his own heart over what he did in life.

Why do I bring all this up - because there is a strong possibility that the government will pass the Freedom of Choice Act early next year. This will make abortions all the more available. In the near future we will put something in the bulletin to enable you to contact your senator or representative to express your position of this Act. It's not my role to tell people who to vote for or what candidate to favor. But as a moral leader I have the responsibility to speak about moral issues and abortion is certainly one of the major ones that we cannot ignore. People ask me why do I not speak about it more. I feel the focus of my homily should always be on God's Word in the Scriptures and, if people respond to what God tells us, then most moral problems will be answered. The miracle of Mary's conception in today's gospel inspired me to say something about the miracle and the gift of life itself. It must be honored and respected in all its stages - from conception to natural death. Amen.

Christmas

December 25, 2008

HOMILY – (Isaiah 62:11-12; Titus 3:4-7; Luke 2:15-20) I read the children's book: *The Invisible String* by Patrice Karst. Because of copyright laws it would not be permissible to reprint the whole story. The theme of the book is a mother explaining to her two small children (who were frightened in the night by lightening) that she is always connected to them by an invisible string. No matter where they went they were connected, and they were connected to one another and to their friends the same way. Love is the invisible string that connects us all and keeps us from ever being lonely. It's a beautiful story.

I went to a class this year (a person has to keep learning even after they graduate from school) and the professor began our class with this story. I thought how perfect for Christmas.

Jesus came to tell us about the invisible string that connects us with God, God's love for us. Because God is a pure spirit God, has no body and God is invisible to our eyes. We can only know him by seeing all the beautiful things God made, and by the holy things God has spoken to us through his prophets, but God wanted to do more to convince us of his love. And so God's own Son became human like us to tell us about God and to tell us about God's love - the invisible connection God has with us.

After he taught us about God's love and showed it to us in everything he did, Jesus returned to his Father in heaven to prepare a place for us where we would be with him forever. But just so we would know he hasn't left us alone, he gave us Communion to help us stay united with him and he sent his Holy Spirit to dwell in our hearts.

That invisible string between us and God, the power of his love for us and the sacraments and the Holy Spirit, and the invisible string that unites us with those we love, this gives us a peace and a joy no one can take from us.

Isn't it great that Jesus was born and aren't you glad to know that we are connected with him and he with us. When we pray we tug on that invisible string and he tugs back, so let us continue to celebrate his birth and thank God for sending him to us to be our friend and our savior. Amen.

Holy Family

December 29, 2002

INTRODUCTION – (Sirach 3:2-6, 12-14; Col 3:12-21; Luke 2:22-40) The Christmas season will last for two more weeks. With Joseph taking Mary as his wife and with the birth of Jesus, a new family is founded and it is a holy one. Ben Sirach, who speaks to us in today's first reading, was a teacher in a Jerusalem school nearly 200 years before Christ was born. Sirach's instructions cover topics such as home life, business, courtship and marriage, travel and entertainment. He even offers proper etiquette for entertaining guests or how to behave when invited out. Today's passage deals with our relationship with our parents, the importance of respect and obedience when we're young, and patience and kindness when we get older and they are too. In our second reading, Paul is writing to counteract the heretical teachings of those who thought that salvation was reserved only for those who were members of certain secret cults. He tells us it's the ordinary virtues that everyone knows and anyone can practice that are important; such as compassion, kindness, humility, gentleness, patience, forgiveness and love. Notice the importance he places on religious virtues such as familiarity with the word of God, prayer, singing and thanksgiving. The Greek word for thanksgiving is Eucharistia. When husbands hear Paul talk about wives being submissive to their husbands, they sometimes do not hear what follows. There is a mutual giving and receiving that is needed in marriage.

HOMILY – When the Holy Family is put before us as a model for us to imitate, we feel that is impossible. They are so far beyond us in holiness that imitating them would be like any of us trying to play baseball like

Mickey Mantle or Babe Ruth. Well, we may not be the perfect holy family, but we are a holy family if we are in God's grace. It's God's grace that makes us holy and if the members of our family stay in God's grace, we are a holy family. The only danger we face is becoming spiritually complacent and lazy. We never stay in the same place spiritually, we are either moving forward or backward, and unless we keep trying to grow in God's grace, we will end up slipping backward or even losing grace altogether. As we heard in the second reading, there are no secrets to living and growing in grace. It's just a matter of practicing the ordinary virtues we learned when we were young: kindness, humility, gentleness, patience, etc. Jesus summed them up in his famous answer about the greatest commandment: loving God as much as we can and loving our neighbor as ourselves. The neighbor that we most often neglect is the person or persons closest to us. We too often take each other for granted instead of making time for one another, helping each other, complimenting each other, thanking each other or being patient and forgiving of one another. Good relationships are made up of just so many little things.

I think at times we imagine the Holy Family lived a charmed life without problems or stress. Problems began even before Jesus was born when Joseph was about to break his engagement to Mary. Think for a moment where Jesus was born - not neat and clean like the little mangers we put up in our homes. He was born in a stable that probably was smelly and dirty, maybe damp and cold. In today's gospel we are told about their presenting Jesus in the Temple and offering the required sacrifice according to the law of the Lord. St. Luke is telling us they were poor, they offered the sacrifice of the poor. St. Luke, incidentally, is telling us they observed the laws of their Jewish faith and were obedient to God. We can't be holy and ignore the things God asks of us. As they went to the Temple, surely they were happy to be able to bring their child there. But then an old man came up to tell Mary her heart would some day be broken because of her child. What a chilling prophecy! Shortly after this St. Joseph is told by an angel to get out of the area, that the king is planning on killing their child. So they end up refugees in a foreign land for a few years. The only other event we know of during Jesus' youth was when he was 12 and he was lost in the Temple for three days. What a worry and concern that must have been.

A holy family is not a family without problems or heart aches. It's how we deal with those problems that really matters. We must be faithful to God at all times and we must deal with each other with fairness, kindness, patience and love. May God's blessings be with you and your families today and throughout the coming year.

Mary Mother of God

January 1, 2009

HOMILY – (Num 6:22-27; Gal 4:4-7; Luke 2:16-21) I entertained myself this afternoon looking up information about the new year. I've always wondered how January 1 became New Year's Day. I wondered how other cultures celebrate new year's. I've always known that the Jewish new year begins on Rosh Hashanah which will fall on September 18, 2009. I've always known that the Chinese have their own new year celebration which this year will be Jan. 26, 2009. Because their calendar is a little shorter than ours, the Moslems began two new years' in 2008; one in January and another in December. But I was amazed to see all the other cultures that have their own new year at different times and seasons. January 1 was chosen as the start of the new year by the early Romans in 153 BCE. Prior to that date they celebrated the new year in the spring which seems logical since nature starts to come alive at that time. But in 153 BCE the Roman senate chose January 1 as the beginning of a new year because that was the day when the Roman consuls took office. The date is quite arbitrary. It is said they celebrated with "boisterous joy, superstitious practices and gross orgies." The early Christians made January 1 a day of penance as a reaction against the excesses of the pagans. Eventually it was made a feast of Mary as the "Mother of God." I learned too that many European countries didn't officially make January 1 the start of the new year until the 16th, 17th, and 18th centuries. Now practically all big cities of the world celebrate January 1 even if they have their own new year, like China.

The Church's celebration of the new year is the first Sunday of Advent. It makes little reference to January 1 as the start of a new year as it falls during the octave of Christmas. Christmas is too important a feast for just a one-day celebration, so the liturgy celebrates Christmas solemnly for eight days. After today, the liturgy continues to celebrate Christmas, but less solemnly, until the feast of the Baptism of our Lord. Although the angel had already told Joseph that Mary's son was to be named Jesus, today also recalls the day on which Jesus was circumcised and officially given his name. We might reflect for a moment how respectful we are of this name by which we are to be saved. Pope Paul VI asked that today be observed as a day of prayer for peace, which is so badly needed in today's world.

As we celebrate the beginning of 2009 we are hopeful nations might find a better way than waging war to get along with one another. We are hopeful also that our world will be more just, that life will be respected, that we might enjoy health and happiness. Although we may party at this time of year, we also have a lot of reasons to be here in church, to seek God's help in the coming year, and to thank him for his help in the past.

Mary, the Mother of God and our spiritual mother gives us an example of how to enter into this new year. We are told she reflected on all these events in her heart. What events? The annunciation by the angel, the visit to her cousin Elizabeth, Jesus' birth, the visit by the shepherds and the magi. May we too continue to reflect on them in our hearts. The rosary can help us in this. May we come to know God's support as we move another year closer to the kingdom of his eternal love. Amen.

Feast of the Epiphany
January 4, 2009

INTRODUCTION – (Isaiah 60:1-6; Eph 3:2-3a, 5-6; Matt 2:1-12) 587 years before Christ, Jerusalem was destroyed by the Babylonians. Fifty years later, the Persians (people living in modern day Iran) conquered the Babylonians, and they allowed the Jews to return home. It was a difficult time for the Jews, rebuilding their country 50 years after it had been destroyed. Their Temple was gone. Jerusalem, their city that gave them such pride, was in shambles. The prophet in today's first reading tries to encourage the people and assures them Jerusalem would again be a great city. He sees Jerusalem becoming a light for all the world. People would come from everywhere to visit Jerusalem and to be nourished by the radiant light of God's presence. St. Matthew sees the vision of the prophet fulfilled in the birth of Jesus and the visit of the magi.

HOMILY – There are so many lessons we can learn from the story of the magi. I am going to dwell on only two of them. They are themes that are very dear to St. Matthew's gospel and I want to spend a few moments showing how these themes appear again and again in his gospel.

First is the theme that God wants all people to be saved. The Jews, as God's chosen people, believed they had a monopoly on salvation. The magi were foreigners, not members of God's chosen people, but they represent all nations whom God calls to know him through Jesus. As we read further on in Matthew's gospel we see how this theme is repeated. Although Jesus instructed his apostles not to go into pagan territory when he sent them out to preach, Jesus himself did not hesitate to cure the servant of a pagan, a Roman centurion. He even marveled at the centurian's faith and on that occasion remarked that "many will come from the east and the west and will recline with Abraham, Isaac, and Jacob at the banquet in the kingdom of heaven" while many of the "chosen people" would miss out. In another place he cured the daughter of a Canaanite woman after he challenged her faith. But most of all, the theme of universal salvation comes through clearly in St. Matthew's gospel when Jesus is about to ascend into heaven. He tells his apostles "Go, therefore, and make disciples of all nations, baptizing them in the name of the Father, and of the Son and of the Holy Spirit, teaching them to observe all I have commanded you."

The visit of the magi tells us God has opened up the doors of salvation to all people, but, and this is the second theme, not everyone chooses to enter into God's kingdom. The story of the magi tells us we have to put some energy and time into finding God and entering into eternal life. Entrance into God's eternal kingdom doesn't come automatically. It doesn't even come if we know our religion perfectly but don't live it. The magi came quite a distance, hundreds of miles, probably even over a thousand, to find Jesus. They had to keep searching, even seeking help from the paranoid king Herod and the indifferent Jewish clergy who had all the answers, but not enough interest in finding the messiah themselves. God's kingdom is for everyone, but not everyone comes looking for it and only those who do, find it. It is a theme we find repeated in many of the teachings of Jesus in St. Matthew's gospel. For example, at the end of the Sermon on the Mount, Jesus tells us the person who listens to his words and acts on them is like a person who builds his house on rock, whereas a person who listens to his words but does not act on them is like the person who builds his house on sand. It will end up in ruins. The theme is repeated in a number of parables. Here's eight that come to mind immediately: 1) the sower and the seed, 2) the wheat and the weeds, 3) the buried treasure and the pearl of great price, 4) the parable about two sons, one who told his father he would do the work his father asked of him but didn't and the other who said he wouldn't, but did, 5) the wedding feast where those invited were too busy to come, 6) the parable of the talents where one man didn't do anything with his talent and lost it in the end, 7) the ten virgins, five of whom were prepared when the groom arrived, and five who missed out on the wedding feast because they were not ready for the groom's arrival. 8) Matthew is the only gospel who gives us the parable of the last judgment when those who were kind and good to the needy were rewarded while those who weren't were rejected from the kingdom.

God's word is absolutely contradicted by our modern day culture, which tells us everyone somehow is going to make it into heaven. The story of the magi shows us those who sincerely search for Christ will find him, but unfortunately not everyone is interested in searching for him sincerely. We ask him today to help us not to get lazy or discouraged as we continue seeking him. His light and grace will always guide us. If we faithfully follow that light, we can be confident we will be saved for Christ for he came a long way to find us and suffered much in order to do so. We recall his saving love as we continue our Mass. Amen.

Baptism of the Lord

January 11, 2009

INTRODUCTION – (Isaiah 55:1-11; 1 John 5:1-9; Mark 1:7-11) Many kings, prophets, and holy people served God in Old Testament times, but in four places in the book of the prophet Isaiah, God speaks of someone with whom he is especially pleased. This servant is not identified by name, and because the passages are in poetic form, they are usually referred to as the servant songs. They were written about 500 years before Christ. Perhaps the passages refer to someone who was alive at the time of the prophet but, amazingly, although they were written 500 years before the time of Christ, they describe Jesus so perfectly. At Jesus' baptism, the voice of God is heard, introducing Jesus to the world, as not only his servant, but as his beloved Son.

HOMILY – Today we celebrate the feast of the Baptism of our Lord. Even though it is an event that took place roughly 30 years after Jesus' birth and the coming of the Magi, it is a feast that fits with the theme of Epiphany. Epiphany means to cause something to be seen, to show, to illuminate or manifest. In last week's feast God revealed his son to the world as represented by the magi. God again reveals his son at the baptism by John the Baptist with his declaration from heaven: "You are my beloved son; with you I am well pleased." So, if you think we are a little slow about removing our Christmas decorations, they are still appropriate to the season. On Monday, Ordinary time begins. It is then that the Christmas/Epiphany season is over. Since they are still so beautiful, we may keep a few poinsettia's around for another week or so.

John's baptism was a baptism of repentance. It's hard for us to understand why Jesus, the sinless one, God's Son, came to John for a baptism of repentance. Even John the Baptist had difficulty understanding why Jesus came to him for baptism. As John said "I need to be baptized by you, and yet you are coming to me?" Because it is difficult to understand, various explanations have been offered as to why Jesus was baptized. 1) Some of the early Church Fathers said Jesus went into the water of the Jordan, not in order to be made holy, but to make the water holy so that all the waters of the world would become life giving through the sacrament of baptism. 2) It crossed my mind that another possible reason Jesus went to be baptized was to show us what his baptism would do, that his baptism would bring the Spirit down upon us and we would become God's beloved children. 3) Inauguration is on everyone's mind these days. Perhaps we can see Jesus' baptism as his official inauguration as he began the work the Father had given him. He was ready to proclaim the gospel, the good news, that for those who turned their hearts to God, God's Kingdom was there for them. The Father and the Spirit put their approval on him and would guide him in this ministry to the world.

4) The last possible explanation I have is perhaps Jesus went to be baptized as an example to us that we are

to be baptized in order to become God's sons and daughters. Right before Jesus ascended into heaven he sent his apostles to continue his work (and that by the way is what the word "apostle" means: one who has been sent). He told them: "All power in heaven and on earth has been given to me. Go, therefore, and make disciples of all nations, baptizing them in the name of the Father, and of the Son, and of the Holy Spirit, teaching them to observe all that I have commanded you. And behold, I am with you always, until the end of the age." If these were his last words, as St. Matthew tells us, baptism must be really important to our Lord.

Most of us do not remember our baptism. We don't remember most of the things that happened to us in our earliest year. Yet those are the things that gave direction to our lives: how we were to treat others, what kinds of food we were to eat, how to care for ourselves, how to act in public, how we were to be educated. In taking us for baptism our parents were setting a direction for us, setting us on the path to holiness through faith in Jesus Christ.

Sometimes parents take their child for baptism because they think they should, but they fail to see the life of Christ that baptism gives has to be nourished and to have opportunity to grow. You might have heard the story about the family who took their second child to church for baptism and after the baptism the older child who was three years old sobbed all the way back home. His father asked what was wrong. He said, "the priest said he wanted us to be brought up in a Christian home and I want to stay with you guys."

Baptism gives Christ's life, a life that needs to be nurtured and given the opportunity to grow just like the baby's physical life does. Some more fundamental religions say let the child grow up and get baptized when they're older so they can make their own choice as to what religion they want to belong to. Parents don't do that with anything else that's important. They don't say we won't send you to school and when you're old enough you can decide what you need to learn; or we'll let you eat whatever you want until you're old enough to decided for yourself. Baptism gives God's life and sets the direction for that life. The child, when he or she is grown, will have to make his or her own choice as to if and how much he or she will be faithful to Christ. When they see their children begin to drift away, that's when a lot of parents do some heavy praying. If this happens, don't give up hope for them and don't stop praying.

I feel as if my thoughts have drifted in various directions and I know much more could be said about baptism. I just want to leave you with one thought. Even though most of us may not remember our baptism, we should thank God, for in it he gave us life and the Spirit and he gave us a loving parent or parents to guide us in the ways of God.

2nd Sunday in Ordinary Time

January 18, 2009

INTRODUCTION – (1 Sam 3:3b-10, 19; 1 Cor 6:13-15, 17-20; John 1:35-42) Today's first reading is one of my favorite Old Testament stories. It's about Samuel who lived a little more than 1000 years before Christ. If you've ever read the Old Testament, you may remember there are two books in the Old Testament called Samuel, the first has 31 chapters and the second has 24 chapters. However, only the first 15 chapters of 1 Samuel actually deal with Samuel. The rest of 1 Samuel and all of 2 Samuel deal with King David. In our Sunday readings at Mass, we hear about Samuel only twice in a three-year cycle. Yet Samuel was a person of major importance in the Old Testament. He was a great prophet, he anointed King Saul as Israel's first king, and later he anointed David to be king. He had an unbelievable influence over the religious and political climate of his day.

At the beginning of the book of Samuel, we are told that his mother, Hannah, was unable to have children and she suffered bitterly over the fact that she was barren. She promised God if she had a son she would dedicate him to God, which is what she did. When Samuel was still a young child, Hanna brought him to the Priest, Eli, who attended to the Arc of the Covenant in Shilo. Under Eli, Samuel would be raised and educated for God's service. This is the background to our first reading.

HOMILY – I'm sure we all have received calls that have changed our lives. There are the kind we hope we never receive; i.e., something tragic happening to someone we love. There are also the ones that change our lives in a good way. Some of you may have met a person at a friend's house or a party and you thought, "I would really like to get to know that person better." After exchanging phone numbers, the person gives you a call and as one thing leads to another you become the best of friends. Your life has been changed and you are grateful for it.

Samuel got a call in the middle of the night. His life was changed and so were the lives of all God's people for hundreds of years thereafter, especially since Samuel is the person who established the monarchy and anointed Israel's first two kings. Martin Luther King received a call to the ministry and that led to other calls to struggle in a non-violent way for justice for all the people in our nation. Andrew and another disciple heard John the Baptist point out Jesus and they responded to Jesus' call to "come and see." The next day Peter received his brother Andrew's call to meet Jesus. Their call was not as dramatic as Samuel's was. It's very, very seldom that God calls out our name in the middle of the night as he did Samuel. Usually he speaks to us through others, through a religious person like John the Baptist or even through a relative or friend. Sometimes he speaks through someone we don't like. If we answer when God speaks, our lives will never be the same. Maybe that's why many people avoid quiet prayer. They might hear God say something they don't want to hear. They're comfortable with their life the way it is.

When I felt God was calling me to be a priest, I kept hoping it wasn't true. I hoped I could be like everyone else and get married some day and have children. But somehow God kept putting the idea of priesthood in my mind. Maybe that's why I like this story of Samuel so much. God just kept calling to me until finally I gave in and said to God: "speak Lord, for your servant is listening." I'm glad I answered "yes." Giving up marriage is hard at times, but so is being married hard at times. Being a priest has been very fulfilling in case anyone is thinking about it.

One thing I think is worth noting. Samuel got guidance from Eli in recognizing God's voice. The disciples first received guidance from John the Baptist in recognizing Jesus. At times we think maybe God is saying something to us but we're not sure. It doesn't have to be some big thing like going into religious life. It can be something as simple as volunteering for some kind of service to others or praying a little more. We think, "is this really what God wants?" It's helpful to get some guidance from a person whom we feel we can trust, who is wise and whom we consider as living a good Christian life. God does reach us through others. We see that all through the Scriptures. We see that in the sacraments.

God touches us and speaks to us through others.

As we come together for the Eucharist, Christ is with us in each other. St. Paul just reminded us of this in our second reading – our bodies are members of Christ and temples of the Holy Spirit. Christ is also with us in our prayers and song, in the Scriptures and in Holy Communion. His eternal call to us is to holiness, which we attain to an ever-greater degree as we come to know him and love him.

3rd Sunday in Ordinary Time
January 26, 2003

INTRODUCTION – (Jonah 3:1-5, 10; 1 Cor 7:29-31; Mark 1:14-20) Whenever we think of Jonah we think of his being swallowed whole by a whale. Actually the bible does not speak of a whale but of a great fish. Jonah as you might remember was sent by God to preach repentance to the Assyrians. The Assyrians were an especially warlike, aggressive and merciless nation. Their capital was Nineveh, a city that was located in the northern part of modern day Iraq, 250 miles north of Baghdad on the Tigris River. The northern kingdom of Israel had already been destroyed by the Assyrians when Jonah was written. So you can imagine, the Jews had no love for the Assyrians. When God told Jonah to preach repentance to the Assyrians, (now Assyria was east of Israel), Jonah got into a boat and headed west. He didn't like the job God gave him and he was going to run away from God and the mission he was given. Well, the boat met with a terrible and violent storm and the sailors discerned the storm was caused by Jonah trying to get away from God. So they threw Jonah overboard and Jonah was swallowed by the fish. Three days later he was deposited on the shore. This time Jonah decided he better do what God wanted. More amazing than the part about the fish is what we hear in today's first reading. Jonah, begrudgingly, converted the entire city of Nineveh in one day, without miracles, spectacular signs or lengthy exhortations. To get an idea of how amazing this would be, think of some little known individual today showing up in Baghdad and in one day every person in Baghdad, from Saddam on down, reforms and converts to Christianity. Wouldn't that be something!!! Most scholars do not consider the book of Jonah as historical, but they treat it more as a parable, taught to teach spiritual truths. Today's section shows God holds out to all people, even to the enemies of the Jews, the chance to reform. Jonah represented the Jewish resentment over this possibility. The passage prepares us for the gospel when Jesus begins to preach repentance. The gospels describe more realistically that calling people to change is not as easy as the story of Jonah makes it appear to be. Jesus begins to gather disciples who will help him in his work.

HOMILY – We have a number of words in the English language that come from the Greek word for time, Chronos. There is chronology, chronicle, chronometry and even chronic which refers to something that lasts a long time. Chronos tells us what time it is. It is e.g. January 26, 2003 at 8:15 a.m. However the Greeks had a second word for time which was Kairos. Kairos meant another kind of time which we might call occasion or opportunity. It tells us what it is time *for*. It's what a mother might mean when she tells her child "it's time for you to get working on your homework." Or we might be thinking now "it's time for spring to come." Or some people might start thinking if I get too long: "It's time to get this sermon over with so

I can go home and watch TV."

In our first reading it was time for the people of Nineveh to reform their lives and do penance. St. Paul tells us in the second reading "time is running out." He was encouraging the Corinthian community to be detached from the things of this world, even marital love, because he expected the second coming of Christ and the end of the world to happen in a very short time. It didn't happen when they expected it to, however, although we do not know when it will happen, Paul's basic idea is absolutely true. We must not get so preoccupied with everyday concerns that we forget about the life that is to come. Salvation is not automatic and we don't have forever to get ourselves ready for it. It's not just old people who die. I know from much experience that death can come to any one at any time. The only thing we can build our lives on that is reliable and permanent is the life we hope to enjoy with God in eternity. Jesus tells us the same thing. "This is the time of fulfillment. The kingdom of God is at hand. Repent and believe in the gospel." Jesus uses the word Kairos when he said "This is the time..." Now is the opportunity for grace. Now is the season to open ourselves to God's life. This is the third of the new mysteries that the Holy Father added to the rosary, called the Mysteries of Light: Jesus' call for conversion. And this call is not just a message for <u>other</u> people to hear. Conversion is ongoing. We all sin. We all tend to get lazy, we all tend to get our priorities out of order at times and put aside the more important things for things that are easier or more fun. And we all have room to grow more in our faith. Opportunities, as we all know, do not hang around forever. So it is <u>now</u>, not tomorrow, not when I turn 80 or 90 years old, <u>now</u> it is time for me to open my life more to Jesus and to the gospel.

And perhaps the Lord is inviting us, as he did Peter and Andrew, James and John, to help get this message out to others. You don't have to be a priest or religious to do this (although right now we can use a few more good priests or religious). Certainly, whoever you are, you can pray for the conversion of someone or you can perhaps even do more to help someone come to our Lord.

The next time you look at your watch, don't just see what time it is, but thank God for the precious gift of time and ask yourself are you using it as best you can. And we couldn't do better than what we're doing right now – praying the most perfect prayer there is: the Mass.

4th Sunday in Ordinary Time
February 1, 2009

INTRODUCTION – (Deut 18:15-20; 1 Cor. 7:32-35; Mark 1:21-28) If you are married, our second reading from Paul's letter to the Corinthians might be difficult for you to understand. So I would like to give a little background to today's second reading. The passage comes from a section of the letter where Paul is answering one of several questions he received in a letter from the Corinthians. This question is about marriage. Somehow the Corinthians decided marriage was not a holy thing and it would be better to live a life of celibacy. In Paul's answer he first affirmed the value of marriage. However, though he stressed it is not for everyone, he also wanted to affirm the value of celibacy. In today's passage he is addressing those who were not yet married or who were widowed and points out the advantages of remaining in such a state. The early Church, including Paul, thought Jesus was going to return very soon and the world would come to an end. To quote Paul, he said, "time is short" and "the world as we know it is passing away." If it sounds as if Paul is overemphasizing the spiritual advantages of celibacy, consider how you might view things in your life if you thought that in a very short time the world would end and Jesus' return was immanent. Your priorities would probably change considerably.

Now let me shift back to today's first reading. Moses and God's people had finally arrived at the Promised Land after several generations of slavery in Egypt and a long journey through the desert. Moses knew that God was calling him to leave this world and God's people would cross the Jordan and enter the Promised Land without him. Basically he is saying "goodbye and good luck." He assures them God would not leave them without direction or leadership. God would send them another prophet like himself who would speak God's word to them. We usually think of a prophet as a person who foretells the future and sometimes the prophet did, but the best definition of a prophet is at the end of today's first reading: one who speaks God's word. Our first reading prepares us for the gospel where Jesus speaks God's word with power and authority.

HOMILY – Moses promised, "A prophet like me will the Lord, your God raise up for you from your own kin; to him shall you listen." God did raise up many prophets but none could compare with Jesus. Jesus spoke God's word as Moses said he would, but Jesus was even more than someone who spoke God's word, he was God's Son. When Moses said "to him shall you listen," he was not foretelling the future, on the contrary, he was telling God's people what they should do. Often they refused to listen. In this way Jesus experienced the same fate as the other prophets.

From the beginning of Mark's gospel, St. Mark wants us to know who Jesus is. He introduced his gospel with the words: "the beginning of the gospel of Jesus Christ, the Son of God." Within a few verses we hear the testimony of John the Baptist that Jesus would baptize with the Holy Spirit. A few verses later Mark tells us that at Jesus' baptism a voice came from the heavens saying to Jesus: "You are my beloved Son. With you I am well pleased." Now, not yet even halfway through Mark's first chapter, he gives us more information about Jesus, but from an unexpected source, the devil. The people in the synagogue recognize the power in Jesus' teaching and that he is a prophet; that is, he speaks the word of God with a freshness and a power they had never seen before. But the devil is no dummy. The devil catches on immediately. The devil cries out from the person who is possessed: "I know who you are – the Holy One of God." The devil is not only perceptive and clever but would remember everything. The devil would remember the announcement of the angels to the shepherds when Jesus was born: "Today in the city of David a savior has been born for you who is Christ and Lord." The devil would have remembered the visit of the magi when Jesus was born. This is the first miracle St. Mark tells us about. He not only wants us to know who Jesus is but he wants us to know Jesus was not afraid of the evil powers in this world and was willing to face them head on. Let me conclude with two ideas:

1) Jesus is admired by many people today. He is considered a good person, a person who cared greatly about others and a great teacher. The Moslems even consider him a great prophet. But that's all he is in the minds of many people. We, as Christians, see him differently. He is not someone whom we can choose to follow or ignore depending on whether we agree with him or not. He is the Holy One of God; he is God's Son. When he speaks to us, as Moses said, we shall listen to him. (Not that we always do, but it's what we should do.

That's one of the reasons why we come to Mass on Sunday. The whole first part of the Mass focuses on hearing the word and reflecting on it.)

2) The devil: We don't hear much about the devil except in jokes. But the devil is not a joke. The Scriptures take him seriously. Some sicknesses such as epilepsy or mental illnesses had been attributed to the devil in past centuries. We now believe they have other causes. In my experience as a priest and counselor, I definitely believe there are evil powers at work in the world, which are called devils. I've never had any dramatic experiences like in today's gospel or like the movie The Exorcist, which, by the way was, in most respects, based on a true story. I am convinced the devil never takes a vacation or a day off. The devil doesn't even need to sleep at night. Mostly I believe the devil is at work, and we don't even know he's there. He helps us in our weaknesses to make the wrong choices. For example, if we're envious, the devil gives us suggestions to help us give in to that trait, and the same with other weaknesses, such as hatred, out of control anger, laziness, pride, lust, greed, gluttony, etc. But there is one stronger than the devil and who can help us if we listen to him. Amen.

5th Sunday in Ordinary Time

February 8, 2009

INTRODUCTION – (Job 7:1-4.6-7; 1 Cor 9:16-19.22-23; Mark 1:29-39) Today in our first reading we hear Job lamenting his sufferings. Depression really is evident when Job says, "I shall not see happiness again." Hopelessness is one of the major characteristics of depression. Whether Job was a real person on not, no one can say for sure, but the Book of Job definitely expresses a feeling we've all felt at times, that life is unfair. At the time this book was written, the view God's people had was that if we are good, all will go well, and if we're not, all kinds of terrible things will happen to us. We all know life doesn't always work that way. The book of Job probes this problem without coming to a satisfactory answer. The author could only conclude God somehow must know what he's doing because we do not. However, even though Job despaired of ever being happy, his misfortunes were reversed in the end and he did die happy.

Our second reading is difficult to understand without knowing the context. Paul is not usually given to boasting, but here he is using himself to inspire the Corinthians to follow his example. The situation at Corinth he is addressing concerned eating meat sacrificed to idols. There were those who thought there was no problem because idols were not really gods anyway. However, this created scandal for other Christians and it was a source of division. Paul said, the first group are theologically correct, but they should forego the right to eat meat sacrificed to idols for the sake of love for their brothers and sisters who did not understand and for the sake of unity. Then he speaks of himself, which we will hear, saying he has given up certain rights he could claim, including the right to be paid for his work, so that he could win more people to the gospel of Christ.

HOMILY – Our gospel tells us about Jesus who was kept busy trying to cure the ills of the world. Notice how important prayer was to him. He needed to gain strength from his Heavenly Father, as we all do, in order to deal with everyday challenges.

I would like to focus on Paul today because I think the second reading connects with certain issues in the Church today. One of the major problems Paul had to deal with in the Corinthian community was trying to keep everyone in union with one another and with Christ. Not only did this problem show itself in the issue of eating meat sacrificed to idols, but unity was threatened when those blessed by various gifts of the Spirit were thinking they were better than everyone else. There were problems with the celebration of the Eucharist. They celebrated in the context of a meal and those well off ate well while the poor didn't have enough to eat. So Paul said: do your eating and drinking at home and not when you gather for the Eucharist. There were other issues too, but especially one stood out. There was a man living in sin with his father's wife. It was so offensive not even pagans would do something like that. Paul said he should be put out of the community until he came to his senses – to be excommunicated. It was a punishment meant to lead him to repentance.

The Church, as any society, has the authority to decide who has gone too far and is no longer a part of the community. This week there was a lot about excommunication in the news. About 25 years ago an Archbishop in France, Archbishop Lefebvre, decided he didn't like all the changes in the Church and started his own Church which is called the Society of St. Pius X. He wouldn't claim he was starting his own Church. He would say the Pope and Bishops and people who changed with Vatican II were all wrong, and he was right, that he was the authentic Roman Catholic. He started ordaining priests who agreed with him and, eventually, after he ignored Pope John Paul II's order to stop, he was excommunicated. In addition, Church Law, also called Canon Law, states if anyone is ordained bishop without the consent of the Holy Father, that person is automatically excommunicated. Four such bishops in the Society of St. Pius X were in this situation and they have repeatedly requested that the excommunication be removed. In his effort to reunite the Archbishop Lefebvre group with the Church, the Holy Father lifted the excommunication on January 21, (two and one half weeks ago.) This does not mean the Society of St. Pius X is now part of the Roman Catholic Church. It only means the penalty has been lifted on these four bishops, but there is a lot that needs to be done before there is full unity. The followers of Archbishop Lefebvre must fully recognize the validity of Vatican II and the Magisterium of the Holy Father.

To complicate things, on the same day the excommunication was lifted, there was a TV interview with one of those bishops, Bishop Williamson, where he denied the Holocaust ever took place. The pope has denounced the position of that bishop and so has the head of the Lefebvre group. Several people have asked me this week how the Holy Father could remove the excommunication from someone who denied the Holocaust. I have tried to make it clear that the excommunication imposed upon the bishops and the lifting of the excommunication was totally unrelated to Bishop Williamson's position on the Holocaust. First of all, the Holy Father did not know Bishop Williamson's position on the Holocaust when he removed the excommunication. Secondly, a person is not excommunicated for saying something so profoundly ignorant. If a person were to remain adamant in that ignorance and were ordered to recant, and they persisted, they could perhaps be excommunicated. I don't know if that could happen here; however, the Holy Father has subsequently demanded that "Bishop Williamson must absolutely, unequivocally and publicly distance himself from his views concerning the Shoah" (the Holocaust) before he could ever be fully united with the Catholic Church as a bishop. As we can see, unity is not easy to achieve. If it were easy, there would not be hundreds of Christian denominations in existence today. The Holy Father asks our prayers for the Church and for himself. Amen.

6th Sunday in Ordinary Time
February 13, 2000

INTRODUCTION – (Lv 13:1-2, 44-46; 1 Cor 10:31-11:1; Mark 1:40-45) One of the jobs of priests in the Old Testament was to act like a dermatologist and decide whether a person with a certain skin disease could be contagious. Whatever the disease was, if it was judged contagious it was called leprosy. The disease we hear about in today's first reading appears to be something like ringworm. If it was decided a person had leprosy, the diseased person was suddenly homeless, without job or family. He or she had to live outside the city, could not associate with relatives or friends, they had to warn people when they were approaching, their home was tombs or caves and they made their living by begging from those traveling to or from the city or town. It would be a horrible sentence to have to condemn someone to. On the other hand, if the priest made the wrong decision and left the person stay around, he could jeopardize the health of the whole community. I'm glad I wasn't a priest way back then. For two chapters the book of Leviticus lays out rules on how to deal with leprosy. Today's first reading is a small section from this part of Leviticus. The rules were harsh, but in those primitive times they were necessary for the survival of the community. This reading is meant to prepare us for the gospel where we see that the power of Jesus and his love deals with sickness in a different way. He reaches out to the isolated and sick person and restores both their health and their ability to be reinstated in community. It is something of an irony that he ends up isolating himself because people gave him no rest.

HOMILY – This story comes from Chicken Soup for the Soul. It was a bitter cold evening in northern Virginia many years ago. An old man stood by a shallow river waiting for someone to come along who could give him a ride across the river. There was no footpath. As he waited, half frozen, along came several riders galloping toward him. He let the first one go by without an effort to get his attention. Then another passed by, then another. Finally, as the last one approached, the old man caught the rider's eye and said, "Sir, would you mind giving an old man a ride to the other side? There's no passage way by foot." Reining his horse, the rider replied, "Sure. Hop aboard." Seeing the old man was too cold and stiff to climb up on the horse, the horseman dismounted and helped the old man up. The rider took the old man not just across the river, but to the old man's home, which was just a few miles away. As they neared his tiny cottage, the rider's curiosity caused him to inquire, "Sir, I noticed that you let several other riders pass by without making an effort to secure a ride. Why did you let all the others pass you by and wait for me to ask me to take you across? What if I had refused and just left you standing there?" As the old man lowered himself down from the horse, he looked the rider in the eye and replied, "I've been around these here parts for some time. I reckon I know people pretty well. I looked into the eyes of the other riders and immediately saw they had no concern for my situation.

It would have been useless to even ask them for a ride. When I looked into your eyes, kindness and compassion were there. I knew you would be willing to help me." The rider replied, "Thank you for your kind words. I hope I'm never too busy that I fail to respond to the needs of others with kindness and compassion." With that, Thomas Jefferson turned his horse around and made his way back to the White House.

Thomas Jefferson is getting some nasty press these days. I thought it would be refreshing to hear something positive about him. I thought this would be a good story for Valentine's day too. There are lots of ways to show love, and most of the love that this world is in need of is not the romantic sort, despite the media's preoccupation with just this one kind.

Today at Mass we celebrate a love that reaches out to us, a love that is infinite, a love that was willing to come down, not from a horse, but from his throne on high as Son of God and put on the weakness of our human flesh, a love that was powerful enough to heal the sick and raise the dead, a love that restored to a poor leper not only his health, but his home and his family and in so doing he made himself unclean by Jewish law because he touched a leper and made himself unable to mingle with others because he was so much in demand. His is a love that was willing to give everything to those he loved, even his own life. But the good news is that the evil powers that took his life did not succeed in the end, for the gift of his life brought about resurrected life for all who believe in him. His love was too powerful to be crushed. And in his love he continues to give himself as food and drink for those who believe in him; not just any food and drink but a food and drink that will give eternal life.

Today we come to the origin and source of all love with our own failures and sins that get in the way of our own ability to love. With the pain we have caused and with the scars from wounds inflicted on us, we ask for healing. Wherever we need healing, in our bodies, in our hearts, in our ability to be more loving toward others, we ask the Lord to reach out and touch us and say to us "be healed."

7th Sunday in Ordinary Time

February 20, 2000

INTRODUCTION – (Is 43:18-19, 21-22, 24b-25; 2 Cor 1:18-22; Mark 2:1-12) When the Jews entered the Promised Land, they entered a land already inhabited by a pagan people known as the Canaanites. The Canaanite worship was filled with superstition and immoral sensuality and was a constant temptation to the Israelites. In comparison to these pagan fertility rites, worship of Yahweh was dull and the people often grew weary of their own God. But their disloyalty to God and their neglect of the Ten Commandments sapped the nation's strength and in their weakness they were eventually defeated by the Babylonians in 587 BC. Not only did the Babylonians defeat them, but they took most of their citizens into exile in the land of Babylon (which is Iraq today.) For almost 50 years God's people remained as exiles. The prophet we hear from this morning was chosen by God to announce that their exile was about to come to an end. From the viewpoint of secular history this would occur through Persia's destruction of Babylon and the decree of the king of Persia in 538 BC that the Jews free to return home. But through the eyes of the prophet who saw with eyes of faith, this was all God's doing. God says, "See, I am doing something new." This was so obvious to the prophet that he asks the people: "do you not perceive it?" Implicit in this return was the message that God was forgiving the past sins of his people. They had learned to turn back to God while they were in Babylon and now they would return home as a new people, their sins forgiven. When God forgives us he makes us a new person, a truth we also see in today's gospel.

The second reading is a bit hard to understand, but it will make a little more sense if we realize Paul is defending himself against the charge of being wishy-washy.

HOMILY – The homes of people in Galilee were simple, probably not much bigger than a two car garage. Their roofs were flat, made of twigs and beaten earth or flat rocks supported by wooden beans. Sometimes they would sleep on the roof at night if it was too hot in the house. It would not have been too hard of a task to make a hole in the roof of the house where Jesus was. But making that hole and lowering their friend to a spot in front of Jesus certainly showed their determination to get the paralyzed man to Jesus. Jesus was always impressed with sincere and persistent faith. "Seeing their faith, Jesus said to the paralytic, 'Child, your sins are forgiven'. "

It probably seems strange to most of us that Jesus began to heal the man by first forgiving his sins. The Jews believed that all suffering was caused by sin, but Jesus knew it was not true all the time. For example when Jesus and his apostles came upon a man born blind, he clearly said in that case no one sinned, neither the blind man nor his parents. But maybe the man in today's gospel needed to be healed spiritually before he could be healed physically. There is a whole area of scientific study that has revealed how closely our spiritual, emotional and physical health are interconnected. It is the study of psychoneuro-immunology; a word that describes how our mental and emotional health affects our immune system. Only God would have known if there were any necessary connection between sin and physical health in the case of the man in today's gospel. At any rate I think there are two obvious things this gospel teaches us, first that Jesus came to destroy evil in all its forms, not just sickness, but sin, the devil, hatred, revenge, and all the other things that are destructive of God's masterpiece of creation: the human person. God does want to make all things new, and the first step Jesus took in making this man a new person was to reconcile him with God. The second important lesson in today's gospel is that Jesus has power to forgive sin. That's not new to us, but it was shocking to them. That he was Son of God had not yet been revealed. The onlookers knew him as a very special man by his teachings and healings. Jesus himself identifies himself as "Son of Man." And his miracle demonstrated to all who were there that this man had a power that was divine, a power not only to heal but to forgive sins. This was a power that he would later share with his apostles and with their successors. This was indeed something new.

I wonder what some of us would have said to Jesus if we were that paralyzed man lying before him. Would we have been grateful to have heard "Your sins are forgiven?" Would we have been happy to hear him say that? How many of us would have thought "is that all you have to offer?" When we had a healing service here with Fr. Rookey, almost two years ago, on a hot summer night, our church was packed and it lasted for three hours. And the same was true in two other churches we went to. I thought it was great, of course, and I'm glad so many came with faith asking for healing. But when we have a reconciliation service, we have maybe 35 or 40 people. Have people stopped committing sins? If that's true I'm glad. I can't claim to be that good. Or maybe we're all much more worried about our physical health than we are about our spiritual health? There are many ways a person can be paralyzed other than being physically paralyzed: the lonely, the depressed, those bored with life, the addicted, the perennially angry and vengeful, and the ordinary person like you and I who still have areas of our lives that we struggle to open to God's grace. What Jesus says to the man on the mat he says to us, rise, pick up your mat and walk! One of the most common laments I hear from people who feel paralyzed is that they can't change. No one need be trapped not even by physical limitations. I hope I won't bore you if I give you a few examples to show that limitations do not need to paralyze us. Helen Keller who was both deaf and blind came out of her shell and became a great inspiration to many. Woody Allen flunked motion picture production at New York University, Lucille Ball was told by the head of the John Murray Anderson Drama School, "Try any other profession, any other." In 1962 four young nervous musicians played for the executives of Decca Recording Co. While turning down this rock group who called themselves the Beatles, one executive said, "We don't like their sound. Groups of guitars are on the way out." When Alexander Graham Bell invented the telephone in 1876, and he made a demonstration call to the President Rutherford Hayes, the president said: "That's an amazing invention, but who would ever want to use one of them?" One of Thomas Edison's teachers in Port Huron complained about him that he was 'too slow.' John Milton became blind at age 44. Sixteen years later he wrote the classic Paradise Lost. The German composer Beethoven had become completely deaf by age 46. Yet he wrote his greatest music, including five symphonies, during his later years, including one we love to sing, the Ode to Joy. Franklin D. Roosevelt was paralyzed by polio at the age of 39. He was elected president of the U.S. four times. John Newton, the Methodist minister who wrote Amazing Grace, was at one time a captain of a ship that dealt in the slave trading business. General Douglas McArthur had to apply to West Point three times. The first two times he was turned down. Abraham Lincoln entered the Blackhawk War as a captain. By the end of the war he had been demoted to the rank of private. The greatest example of all is Jesus Christ who overcame the power of death because he was faithful to the Father in heaven. And he gives us the confidence we too can overcome even death by sharing in his risen life, a life that comes to us through our union with him. God is making us into a new creation in himself. "See," God says, "I am doing something new…do you not perceive it?" Our union with him depends on sanctifying grace, a precious gift given to us at baptism, strengthened at confirmation and nourished through prayer, the Eucharist and the sacrament of reconciliation when we need it. Today he tells us as he told the paralytic "rise, pick your mat, and walk," walk in faith, hope and love and in the newness of life grace gives us. Amen.

1st Sunday of Lent

March 1, 2009

INTRODUCTION – (Gen. 9:8-15; 1 Peter 3:18-22; Mark 1:12-15) A covenant typically is a serious commitment or promise two people make to each other. It defines their relationship and the expectations they have of each other. Except when people get married, the word "covenant" is not often used today. However, before the time of Christ, it was the usual manner by which people, and sometimes nations, entered into binding agreements with one another. It was the way God chose to enter into a relationship with his people. During this season of Lent, the theme of covenant will keep coming up in the weeks to come. Today we hear about the covenant God made with Noah and all creation after the great flood. Notice this covenant is unusual in that God makes all the promises and asks nothing of Noah and his family in return. St. Peter, in the second reading, tells us this covenant prefigured baptism with God promising us salvation and eternal life. As we shall learn in the weeks to come, God does have expectations of us. Whenever we come to Mass, we renew this covenant God has made with us. We are assured of eternal life through Jesus Christ, and we commit ourselves to loving and obeying him.

HOMILY – In Arthur Miller's play, *Death of a Salesman*, the central character is Willy Loman, an aging salesman who has been forced to work only on commission. His meager income can't pay the bills. Yet he refuses to face reality. He struggles to keep the illusion that he is highly successful and greatly loved by all his customers. Eventually he loses his job and decides to end his life, which he does. His son said of his father, "he never knew who he really was."

Who are we? Answering who we are is often best answered when we know what we are looking for in life? What do we want most out of life? I've just finished reading a wonderful book: *The Seven Storey Mountain* by Thomas Merton. Thomas Merton grew up pretty much without any relationship with God. He struggled to find happiness and peace in life but couldn't seem to find it anywhere, not until he found his way into the Catholic

Church and ultimately to the Trappist Monastery near Bardstown, Kentucky. He found himself, he found who he was, in finding God.

I am reminded of a retreat I made about 30 years ago. It was a guided retreat where I met with the retreat master for an hour every day. The retreat master asked me to reflect on the question "What do you want most in life?" Being younger as I was, my answer to myself was immediate: I thought I would be happiest if I could have a beautiful, young, loving wife (maybe rich too!). Even as a priest I couldn't help envying couples I would happen to see together, wishing I could have been the one holding hands with the loving wife. It seemed like the right answer to the question, "What do you want most in life?" But the question continued to reassert itself throughout the three days of retreat, continued to seek an answer as if it had not been answered at all. On the last day of retreat, I was praying in church. Looking deep into my soul, I discovered the real answer to that question, an answer that gave me the greatest peace, a peace that has held up in almost all the difficulties I've faced since then. The real answer to the question, "what do I want most in life?" was "to be and to do whatever God wanted of me." I realized if I did that, my life would be a success. That peace was tested and demonstrated itself almost immediately. When I left the church, apparently there was a couples' retreat going on at the retreat house, and lots of couples were walking around talking and holding hands. I felt very peaceful about it, watching them, happy for them and not feeling any envy at all, or wishing I were anything other than what I was. The natural yearning for love and companionship and intimacy didn't disappear that day, but I experienced a new peace in dealing with it.

What was Jesus doing in the desert? He didn't need to

do penance for any misdeeds. Perhaps he was asking himself the same questions: Who am I? What do I want in life? What does God, the Father, want of me?

The next forty days invite us to our own time of retreat. Maybe we can't get away for a few days, but maybe we can find some way to ask our self, what am I looking for in life? What are the temptations that keep me from knowing God better, knowing myself better? Jesus tells us: "The kingdom of God is at hand." It's right in front of us, if we only have eyes to see and ears to hear.

2nd Sunday of Lent
March 8, 2009

INTRODUCTION – (Gen 22:1-2, 9-13, 15-18; Rom 8:31-34; Mark 9:2-10) Last week we heard about God's covenant with Noah. Another important covenant is implied in today's first reading - God's covenant with Abraham. God promised Abraham numerous blessings, including many descendants. In return, God asked Abraham simply to trust him. Today we hear how Abraham remained trusting in a most difficult situation. Abraham must have felt great anguish when he sensed God was asking him to sacrifice his beloved son, Isaac. I often wonder if God really asked this of Abraham or if Abraham just thought God was asking this of him. Human sacrifice was common in many cultures, including that of Abraham's closest neighbors, so it was natural that Abraham may have thought he should make this kind of sacrifice just as others were doing.

HOMILY – One cold winter evening a priest was walking through a dangerous neighborhood. A man hiding in the shadows didn't recognize him as a priest because the priest had his topcoat buttoned up to his chin. The man came out of the shadows with a gun and asked the priest to give him his wallet. When the priest opened his coat to get it, the man with the gun saw his Roman collar and apologized. He said "Sorry Father, I didn't know you were a priest. I can't steal from you. Just go on your way." The priest was so relieved he reached into his coat pocket and pulled out a cigar. He said "Thank you my good man. Let me give you a cigar." The robber said "I appreciate that Father, but I can't take it. I gave up smoking for Lent."

Well, the obvious point is that whatever spiritual practice we choose to take on during Lent, it is supposed to change us, it is supposed to make us better people. Changes come in many ways. Some are good, some are not. Some are gradual, some occur with amazing speed. Today's readings deal with the most profound change any human will ever face: the end of life in this world and the beginning of life in the next. Did you notice how the themes of death and life are part of each of today's readings?

Abraham's son Isaac came within seconds of having his life taken from him, but he was spared. His having been spared was like a resurrection for him. Abraham's relief in his son's remaining alive would have been enormous.

St. Paul reminds us that Jesus' death and resurrection is an assurance of God's love.

In the gospel, Jesus' transfiguration is not only a revelation of divine glory hidden in Jesus, but the transfiguration is closely tied to Jesus' death and resurrection. If you go to St. Mark's gospel and read the passage immediately preceding the account of the transfiguration, you will see that right before Jesus went up the mountain, Jesus warned his apostles that he would be put to death and would rise again. Immediately after the event, when coming down from the mountain, he tells Peter, James and John, who were with him during the transfiguration, not to tell anyone what they had experienced until he had risen from the dead.

Our season of Lent prepares us to celebrate again what Jesus has done for us in his death and resurrection. We are called to enter into new life with him now so that when our time comes we can enter fully into his glory. Some day, as Jesus was changed, we too will be changed if we remain in union with him. If we continue to share in his life through faith, when we lay aside this present life with its joys and sorrows, its triumphs and its weaknesses, we will enter into a glorious new world which Jesus has opened up to us. We too will be transfigured. Amen.

3rd Sunday of Lent

March 15, 2009

INTRODUCTION – (Exodus 20:1-17; 1 Cor. 1:22-25; John 2:13-25) Covenant is a theme that keeps recurring in our first reading these Sundays of Lent. The first Sunday of Lent we hear about God's covenant with Noah. Last Sunday we heard about God's covenant with Abraham and how Abraham's trust in God was tested when he heard God tell him to sacrifice his son. Today, the third Sunday of Lent, we hear about God's covenant with his people as they traveled under the leadership of Moses from slavery in Egypt to the Promised Land. God, for his part of the covenant, promised his people liberty, land, prosperity and his special care and love. Today's first reading tells us what God expected of them in return.

HOMILY – I want to draw for you a mental picture of what Jerusalem looked like at the time of Jesus during the Passover celebration. At that time the activities at the Temple were the year's major event: religiously, culturally and economically for all of Israel, especially for Jerusalem. Jews came to Jerusalem from all over the world at Passover. Josephus, the Jewish historian, may be exaggerating when he says over 250,000 Passover victims - oxen, sheep and doves - were sacrificed during Passover, but certainly the figure ran into many thousands. (Jerusalem in the Time of Jesus, Joachim Jeremias, pg. 57). The Law required that the animals for sacrifice be perfect. Since people came from distant places, which would have been burdensome to bring an animal with them, not to mention risking the possibility their animal would be rejected because it had some imperfection, it was expedient that the great majority of the animals be sold in Jerusalem. With only one place to buy what they needed, they would get no bargains. Are you beginning to get a picture of something like a county fair with people packed together coming and going, moving along with thousands of oxen and sheep, or carrying doves in little birdcages. The high priestly family may have been in on this business big time. Josephus described the High Priest Ananias as "the great procurer of money." (ibidem, pg 49) On top of all this there were the moneychangers.

The law required that people purchase their sacrifice with Jewish currency. Roman coins were considered idolatrous because they were engraved with pagan inscriptions and images. Since the Jews were under Roman occupation, they probably had to use Roman currency in their everyday lives. So when people came to Jerusalem and they wanted to buy an animal for sacrifice, they had to exchange their foreign money for Jewish currency. Thus we have the moneychangers. One wonders how much profiteering was happening as the exchange was made.

Aside from any cheating or dishonesty, there were those who were getting quite wealthy in the name of God. Jesus told the Jewish leaders who challenged him for doing what he did: "you have made it (the Temple) a den of thieves." We sometimes wonder why Jesus reacted so violently in this instance. We see him nowhere else in the Scriptures expressing such anger. Quite possibly he was angry at seeing how poor people coming to worship God were being ripped off. The gospels give us another reason too for his anger as they recalled the psalm verse: "Zeal for your house will consume me." Obviously he placed worship of God much more highly than most people do. We all know how easy it is to become careless in our reverence and devotion to our Heavenly Father. Often God gets put in second place, or even further down in our list of priorities. It was not that way with Jesus. His Heavenly Father always took first place with him.

We heard the Commandments in our first reading. Notice they are not suggestions or recommendations. They are spoken by one who speaks with authority. Notice that our obligations to God are placed at the top of the list. Is that because God is in need of our worship? No, it's just putting things in perspective. If we value our relationship with God, everything else falls into place. When God is forgotten, then we have no anchor, no ground on which to base our morality, no one to whom we are accountable. We make up our own rules; we make ourselves into our own gods. That's where Adam and Eve got into trouble; they wanted to make themselves equal to God and make their own rules. That is how they lost the happiness God initially gave them.

The commandments and the cleansing of the Temple might prompt us today on this third Sunday of Lent to reflect on our own relationship with God. We call him Lord. Do our lives show that we believe what we say?

4th Sunday of Lent

March 22, 2009

INTRODUCTION – (2 Chronicles 36:14-16, 19-23; Eph. 2:4-10; John 3:14-21) Last Sunday we heard about God's covenant with his people as they traveled with Moses from slavery in Egypt to freedom in the Promised Land. God promised his people many blessings and his special love and in return they were to keep his Law, especially the part of the Law we call "The Ten Commandments." The Jewish historian who wrote the book of Chronicles gives us a summary of over seven centuries of infidelities on the part of God's people to their covenant. The consequences of their infidelity led to untold disaster for the nation, but God would not let them be destroyed totally. Just to help you visualize this better, the Babylonians who practically destroyed them came out of modern day Iraq. The Persians who restored them to their land came out of Iran. Our psalm refrain is the lament of God's people as they suffered captivity in Babylon. Next week we will hear Jeremiah promise that God would make a new covenant with his people since the old one was so poorly kept. We celebrate and renew God's new covenant as always as we celebrate the Eucharist today.

HOMILY – Our gospel comes from the third chapter of St. John. The third chapter begins with Nicodemus coming to talk with Jesus. We only hear about Nicodemus from St. John and he comes up three times in John's gospel. He was a Pharisee and a Jewish religious leader, which implies he is one of the 71 members of the Sanhedrin, the supreme ruling council of the Jews.

We have a stained glass window in the room in the back of Church picturing Jesus talking with Nicodemus. We now call it the brides' room, but originally it was the baptistery and the window was placed there because, at this meeting with Jesus that today's gospel is about, Jesus talks with Nicodemus about baptism.

John tells us Nicodemus came to Jesus at night. On a practical level, he was avoiding the possibility that any of his peers (who were hostile to Jesus) might see Nicodemus associating with this preacher from Nazareth. John uses light and darkness all through his gospel as a symbol of truth and error, grace and sin. John was also telling us symbolically that Nicodemus came from the darkness to Jesus, who is the light. John employs this same symbolism after Judas betrayed Jesus. At the Last Supper Judas left the supper room and John tells us when he went out, it was night. He's not so much telling us the time of day but that Judas was walking away from Jesus, the light.

Although Nicodemus was a teacher in Israel, what Jesus had to say to him left him completely perplexed. Jesus told Nicodemus a person must be born again if he or she is ever to see the Kingdom of God. Nicodemus thought Jesus was telling him we had to start over again in life like a little baby. To clarify things for Nicodemus, Jesus explained that simply being born into this world does not entitle us to eternal life. We must be born again of water and the Spirit. This conversation leads us into today's gospel.

Before I get into what our gospel tells us, I want to

digress and mention the other two times when Nicodemus shows up in John's gospel. The second time is later on when the Sanhedrin wanted to convict Jesus of being an imposter and seducing the people into believing he was the Messiah. Nicodemus spoke up and said Jesus should not be condemned without a fair trial. He was, of course, ridiculed for his comments. Lastly we see Nicodemus at he end of Jesus' life when he brought spices to help with Jesus' burial. He obviously grew in courage as he more boldly showed his faith in Jesus. In these three instances we see Nicodemus moving from darkness into the light.

Now back to today's gospel. I am simplifying Jesus' teachings considerably. Jesus goes on to say that his death and resurrection are the basis of the spiritual life to be revealed by him. The words "raised up" in John refer both to Jesus being raised up on the cross and his glorification in his resurrection and ascension. Jesus used an example to explain this that Nicodemus would have understood. The example is taken from an event from the book of Numbers where the Jews, in their journey through the desert, encountered a nest of poisonous snakes. Many were bitten with a painful bite and many died. God, however, told Moses to make a bronze serpent and put it on a pole and all who looked upon it were healed and saved. And so, it is through Jesus' saving death and resurrection and our faith in him, celebrated and expressed through baptism and the Eucharist (which we will see later in John's gospel) that we are saved. Jesus stresses that he has come to save us simply because of God's great love and not because we deserve it or earned it. But he cautions us that his love cannot save us if we do not open ourselves to it. It is like the light, Jesus says. We can choose to open our eyes and hearts to his light or we can remain in the dark, the darkness of life without Christ.

So we hear the famous verse John 3:16: God so loved the world, God so loved you and me, that he sent his only son who died and rose to give us life. This is the new covenant that God offers us. We recall that love and express our faith in his love now as we celebrate our Eucharist. Amen.

5th Sunday of Lent
March 29, 2009

INTRODUCTION – (Jeremiah 31:31-35; Hebrews 5:7-9; John 12:20-33) The prophet Jeremiah lived 600 years before Christ. He was sent by God to mercifully warn God's people that they were living on the edge of catastrophe. If they didn't start following God's ways the Babylonians would invade their land and destroy them. Centuries of wanton idolatry and social injustice had seriously demoralized and weakened God's people. If they followed what God was telling them through Jeremiah they could avoid disaster. Of course, they ignored Jeremiah and punished him for his message. Today's first reading comes shortly before the Babylonian invasion. God speaks, through Jeremiah, that he is gravely disappointed with the way God's people continually violated the covenant they made with God at Mt. Sinai, a covenant Moses solemnly sealed in blood centuries earlier. In spite of their unfaithfulness, God still loved his people and would make a new covenant with them. Six hundred years later, Jesus used these words "new covenant" when he gave the cup of his blood to his apostles at the Last Supper. We renew that covenant with him each time we come to Mass.

HOMILY – Today's gospel is from John chapter 12,

verses 20 to 33. If you would look at verse 1 of this chapter, John tells us it was six days before Passover and Jesus had just arrived in Bethany, a little town located on the Mount of Olives just across the Kidron valley from Jerusalem. Jesus was going there to celebrate Passover that year, just as thousands of other Jews were doing. That year Passover began on Friday evening, so six days before meant Jesus arrived in Bethany sometime on Saturday. Some of his friends, including Martha, Mary, and Lazarus, prepared a dinner for him - not necessarily at their home. It would have to have been a big dinner – remember Jesus had 12 apostles with him. Lazarus, some time before as you know, had been raised from the dead by Jesus, an event that led many Jews to believe in Jesus. While at this dinner, Mary anointed Jesus' feet with expensive perfume. Judas registered a complaint that the gesture was wasteful and the perfume should have been sold so the proceeds could have been given to the poor. Judas, John tells us, was the treasurer for the group and he didn't care for the poor but used to steal from the money with which he had been entrusted. Jesus told Judas to "leave her alone. She did it in preparation for my burial." And, indeed, Jesus would be buried before the week was over.

John tells us that the next day, which would have been the first day of the week, news got around that Jesus was going into Jerusalem just a couple of miles from where he was in Bethany. When a crowd heard he was going into the city, they met him with palm branches singing "Hosanna. Blessed is he who comes in the name of the Lord." The Pharisees remarked to each other: "We cannot win! Look the whole world has gone after him." Although we won't commemorate Palm Sunday until next week, I wanted to mention this because the anointing at Bethany and the triumphal entry into

Jerusalem immediately preceded today's gospel and are connected with it, especially the theme of Jesus' death. After the Pharisees commented that the whole world has gone after him, John tells us it's true. Some Greeks showed up wanting to see Jesus and that's where today's gospel begins.

Most scripture scholars believe that it was after Jesus entered Jerusalem on this occasion that he drove the merchants and money-changers out of the Temple. That's where Matthew, Mark and Luke place the cleansing of the temple in their gospels. But John had already told us about that incident earlier in his gospel, so he does not mention it here. Instead, when these Greek worshippers sought to see Jesus, Jesus saw this as a sign that his hour had come. "Hour" is a key word in John. It described the time he would complete his mission here on earth. It was the time when he would be put to death for faithfully fulfilling his work of teaching, healing, forgiving sins and spreading God's love. It was the time when Jesus would be raised up, both on the cross and in the resurrection, a time when God would manifest to the utmost his presence in his Son.

Today's gospel is Jesus' own reflection on his death. Being human it is not something he wants to go through. "I am troubled now," he says. The Greek word used here does not mean something like a mother telling her children "I am troubled when you don't come when I call you." The Greek word means to experience inward turmoil, to be stirred up, disturbed, unsettled, thrown into confusion. He wonders aloud if he should say: "Father, save me from this hour." If he escaped or ran away, he would abandon all that he had done and all he came to do and his good works would be forgotten forever. He had to face this hour so that he could be glorified and God would be glorified in him. Here the word "glory" does not mean Jesus was looking for human praise. "Glory" in the scriptures means a special revelation of God's presence. It means that he would save us through his death, resurrection and ascension. Jesus gave us an example to help us understand how his death would lead to our salvation. Like a seed must die in order to produce a new growth, so through Jesus' death, resurrection and return to the Father new life would come forth in those who have followed him. He tells us, "where I am, there also will my servant be." We will all face death, but following him involves another kind of death, death to selfishness and sin, and maybe even martyrdom. But death to ourselves will lead to life eternal. As Jesus prays for the strength to get through the ordeal ahead and thus give glory to the Father by fulfilling his mission, God the Father's voice is heard. The Father's words give testimony about Jesus. The gospel ends on a note of hope, for this will be a time of judgment for the world. This means it will look as if evil has won with Jesus' death. But Christ's glorification will put an end to the power of evil in this world. (Incidentally I read once this is the idea behind April fools day: it's association with Easter. When Jesus rose, the devil, who thought he got rid of Jesus was made to look a fool.) Evil will not triumph. Jesus will win in the end. We need to keep this optimism in trying times and know that in Jesus is our hope and our life. Amen.

Passion Sunday
April 5, 2009

HOMILY – (Isaiah 50:4-7; Phil 2:6-11; Mark 14:1-15:47) A week's events in the life of Jesus are compressed into one hour today, from the triumphal entry of Jesus into Jerusalem to the Last Supper to Jesus' arrest, crucifixion and burial. Throughout this week we will reflect on these important events in a less hurried way. If we could all get to liturgy on Holy Thursday and Good Friday, we would not need to hear the passion read today, but not everyone can get to church during the week, so we need to hear the passion today so we can celebrate Jesus' resurrection next Sunday.

However, I would urge everyone to read the gospel again this week so you can reflect more deeply on Jesus' sacrifice of himself for us. Every year I ask myself why he did it. Every year I think I understand it a little more and yet it will always remains a mystery. Jesus said he came "to seek out and to save the one who is lost." Could he have done that without having to die? Maybe that's what he agonized over in the garden of Gethsemane, asking himself and his heavenly Father the same question.

We too have our struggles to understand suffering. It's amazing how many people want to blame suffering on God. We know it was part of Jesus' mission and God's plan. He prayed "not my will but thine be done." When problems arise for us does it make sense to think this is God's will for us? A lot of people do. For some it helps them cope with tragedy, while others turn their back on God and claim he is cruel and unfair. If we stop and think about life, so many problems we deal with we create for ourselves, or some other individual uses their God-given gift of free will in a way that damages us, or our problems come just because we're human and we grow old and body parts begin to wear out. Or there are times when it's a matter of bad luck, being in the wrong place at the wrong time. We can't always put our finger on why bad things happen, especially to good people, a question that philosophers and theologians have pondered over for centuries. I believe all good things come from God, but there are precious few of the bad things in life that I attribute to God's will. I believe God came to save us from evil, even physical evil (that's why Jesus healed people and why he told us to care about people who were suffering from not having the necessities of life). I don't even know if God plans when he is going to call each of us to leave this world, but eventually it will happen. It's part of our faith and comforting to know, however, that when it happens, if we have served him faithfully, God will take us to himself.

What keeps me going and helps me stay positive is to believe that when bad things happen that are beyond our control, God can turn them into something good. If God could take the death of Jesus, indeed a very evil thing in that we human beings, created in the image and likeness of God, crucified our God – even though he only helped people and loved people, if God could take that and turn it into something good and make it the source of our salvation and eternal life, then God has the power to turn anything around and make it into something good. Sometimes I ask, "God how are you going to bring something good out of this?" My faith is he can and he will and I believe it because I've experienced this all through my life.

Today we reflect on the mystery of suffering, Jesus' suffering and our own. It's not a problem to solve but a mystery we have to live with. Especially at Mass today, as at every Mass, we recall what Jesus did for us. We do, in his memory, what he commanded us. We are assured that in his sufferings he was there before us, he knows what it's like and he will walk with us through bad times and will pull us through. Christ has died, Christ has risen, Christ will come again. Amen.

Holy Thursday

April 9, 2009

HOMILY – (Exodus 12:1-8, 11-14; 1 Cor 11:23-26; John 13:1-15) Fran told me two weeks ago this is the time of the year when people hang up on her when she calls. That's because for years Fran has been so kind as to recruit people for the foot washing. A lot of people avoid talking to her as we get closer to Holy Thursday. People react like Peter: "Fr. Joe will never wash my feet." Well, I'll admit it is humbling to have your pastor kneel in front of you and wash your feet. For me, though, it's not very humbling at all. I think it's very special. But in Jesus' day it was a different story. It was a dirty job. People in those days didn't wear shoes and socks. They wore something more like sandals, and most people walked when they went anywhere. They walked the same dusty, dirty roads that herds of animals walked on. So you can imagine people's feet were dirty and smelly. Having their feet washed when they went to someone's house for dinner would have been refreshing. But the master of the house didn't do the foot washing. Slaves or servants did that job and where there were no slaves or servants, the children or the wife did it. I suppose if I wanted to be really humble, I would go wash the feet of several homeless people and have no audience or pretty singing while I was doing it. But we do it tonight to dramatize what Jesus did.

One of our candidates for foot washing remarked, "I don't know what to think about this." Well, Jesus did a lot of teaching and a lot of healing and helping people. But this last night with his apostles before his death, he wanted to really do something off the wall that would stick with them and symbolize what he was all about. So he told them how to think about what he had done. He said: "I have given you a model to follow, so that as I have done for you, you should also do." He had previously told us, "Whoever wishes to be great among you must be your servant, and whoever wishes to be first among you must be your slave." He gave us an example of the great commandment of love; that we should love one another as he has loved us.

But there was an interesting interchange between Jesus and Peter. When Jesus came to Peter, Peter basically asked, "why are you going to wash my feet?" Jesus said, "you don't understand now why I'm doing it, you will understand later." Peter protested, "you will never wash my feet." Jesus said (and I like this translation better), "If I do not wash you, you won't belong to me." That is as strong a statement as Jesus could have made. I asked myself why Jesus was so definite and why it was so important that everyone have their feet washed, even Peter? Thinking of what Jesus was doing as a demonstration of service, it struck me that we all need to allow ourselves to let Jesus serve us. In what ways does he serve us? He serves us through his sacrificial death on the cross and his resurrection. In his words, he came to seek out and to save the one who is lost; and that's all of us. It's only when we know we need to be saved that we will really know Jesus for that's what the name "Jesus" means: God saves. How do we make this connection with his saving love? Two ways: prayer and the sacraments. In those two ways Jesus can serve us and save us.

Especially in the Eucharist does Jesus come to us to bring us the love and life he wants to share with us. He makes himself vulnerable to us. We can receive him with love, we can receive him with indifference, we can receive him with distraction, we can be too busy to bother coming to receive him at all. But for those who open the door of their heart to him, he is there to share a meal with us as friends. (Rev. 3:20) What greater gift can he give us than himself. "My flesh is real food and my blood real drink," he tells us in John's sixth chapter on the Eucharist.

Tonight we recall Jesus' last supper with his disciples. He came to serve them and he did serve them as their teacher and Lord, but now he was about to serve them (and all of us) by his death on a cross. He demonstrated to us how we are to serve one another and gave us a command to do so. And at the Last Supper he gave us a way to remember what he has done for us and how he continues to bring us into union with his saving work, the Eucharist. "Do this in memory of me" we hear him say twice in tonight's second reading, the oldest recorded account of the institution of the Eucharist.

We may not understand it all, we may not understand why Jesus had to die to save us, we may not understand how a small host and a sip of wine can bring Jesus to us, we may not even understand why God would love us so much as to send his Son to save us, but as Jesus said to Peter: "you will understand later." Amen.

Good Friday
April 2, 2010

HOMILY – (Is 52:13-53:12; Heb 4:14-16, 5:7-9; John 18: 1-19:42) Every day we gather around this altar to celebrate the Eucharist. In the Eucharist God's love is shown to us through Jesus Christ who gave his life for us on the cross. So he can share his life with us now, he continues to give us his body and blood. The gift of his life involved immense suffering on his part. Our gospels do not dwell long on his sufferings. They didn't need to because the people who lived at the time the gospels were written knew what crucifixion involved. It was one of the most agonizing forms of execution that human beings had ever concocted. On this one day of the year, out of respect for what Jesus went through, we do not celebrate the Eucharist as we do every other day. Instead we have a rather extended service of reflection, intercessions, and Communion.

Rather than focusing on the physical sufferings of Jesus, I would like to reflect on the mystery of suffering itself. The book of Genesis attributes suffering to sin. The first man and woman God created lost the happiness God had intended for them because of their disobedience to God. The whole first part of the Old Testament, Deuteronomy, Judges, Samuel and Kings and many of the prophets reflects this notion of suffering – that it is caused by disobedience to God. There is some truth in that notion, but it is not the whole story as the Book of Job tells us. Without telling us why good people suffer, the Book of Job took issue with the old theology on suffering. Sometime about 500 years before Christ, the prophet Isaiah gave us a new way of thinking about suffering - that it can have a positive purpose – that one person's suffering can bring blessings to another. We heard it clearly expressed in today's first reading from a passage in Isaiah known as the 4th Servant Song. I would like to repeat some phrases from our first reading; they are so powerful. God's Servant, Isaiah says, "was spurned and avoided by people, a man of suffering, accustomed to infirmity…Yet it was our infirmities that he bore, our sufferings that he endured…he was pierced for our offenses, crushed for our sins; upon him was the chastisement that makes us whole, by his stripes we were healed…though he had done no wrong nor spoken any falsehood, the Lord was pleased to crush him in infirmity... he shall take away the sins of many and win pardon for their offenses."

It is easy to see in a family how one person's sufferings can benefit another person. For example, how parents make sacrifices for their children, how they have to go through difficult times to support those they love and teach them and discipline them. The sufferings of Jesus, however, were a scandal to his followers. The Messiah was not expected to suffer. We remember when Jesus tried to warn his disciples that he would "suffer greatly and be killed and would rise again." Peter replied, "Heaven forbid, Lord, this will never happen to you." Jesus response to Peter is familiar to all of us: "Get behind me, Satan."

Why did he have to suffer? I have asked myself that question many times and others have asked me that question many times as well. My current thinking on this is I think he <u>had</u> to suffer because of who he was. He was God's Son who came among a sinful people. He could not be anything other than who he was and, without redemption, we could not be anything other than who we are. He was like a lamb dropped into a tigers' cage. He was from above, we are from this world, his holiness did not fit in with our sinful ways. The only kingdom we could know was the kingdom of this world and his kingdom did not belong to this world. Thus he came to his own and his own received him not. Because he could not be other than who he was and because he was faithful to the <u>purpose</u> for which he came - his purpose being to confront the powers of evil, to heal and to teach us to change our lives and to live in a new way - conflict, confrontation, rejection and suffering were inevitable. Yet his sufferings led to his resurrection and glorification. Jesus has "passed through the heavens," as the Letter to the Hebrews tells us, to take his rightful place at God's right hand. But he has not left us, rather through his Spirit, through prayer and the sacraments and through his love in us he has transformed us and made us sharers in his new life. He has made us into a new creation. "He has become the source of eternal life for all who obey him," the Letter to the Hebrews tells us. Or as Isaiah tells us: "By his stripes we were healed." Amen.

Easter
April 12, 2009

HOMILY – (Acts 10:34, 37-43; Col 3:1-4, John 20: 1-9) This funny story is old, but even if you've heard it before, you might enjoy it again. There was an old couple who argued a lot, and they decided to travel before they died. One place they wanted to see was Israel. While they were there, the wife died. When the husband tried to see what arrangements he could make for her funeral, the mortician told him she could be buried in Israel for $2,000 or they could send her body home to the United States, but it would cost $20,000 to transport her. He thought for a moment and said we'll send her to the United States. A friend asked why he would spend so much money to send her back home. He said, "one time a person rose from the dead here in Israel and I can't take that chance."

Our faith tells us one person did indeed rise from the dead, Jesus Christ, and if it weren't for his resurrection we would never have heard of him. He was a good and holy man who was a wise teacher and a powerful healer but, unlike with other religious leaders, if it weren't for Jesus' actual resurrection, his followers would never have had the courage to preach about him to the world. [for Sunday morning: Remember Peter who denied Christ. We hear him preaching with boldness to a pagan audience in today's first reading.] The apostles had nothing to gain in this world from talking about him except rejection and martyrdom. But they had to proclaim him to the world because they had seen him after the resurrection, he sent them out to continue his work, he promised to be with them and they wanted to be with him and these things they couldn't deny.

Their "good news" about the resurrection spread against all odds, persecution, heresy, sinful leadership and a way of life that demanded unselfishness and self-sacrifice. Their promise was a promise of new life, eternal life, to those who heard the "good news" and believed in it. Their promise was a promise of risen life for those who are born again into Christ's life. We hear Paul proclaim this in today's epistle: "we were indeed buried with him through baptism into death, so that just as Christ was raised from the dead by the glory of the Father, we too might live in newness of life." (Rom 6:4 – from Vigil) This is echoed in our epistle for Easter Sunday from Colossians "You have died, and your life is hidden with Christ in God. When Christ your life appears, then you too will appear with him in glory." (Col 3:3-4 – Easter Sunday).

Our bodies will rise again on the last day, but not all will rise to glory. The bible tells us in the book of Daniel: "Many of those whose bodies lie dead and buried will rise up, some to everlasting life and some to shame and everlasting contempt." (Dan. 12:2) It is not our place to decide which group certain of our acquaintances might end up in. We cannot judge anyone's heart, only God can. It's our place to know that we are saved, not by our own power, but through our union with the glorified and risen Christ and to find peace in knowing that God's mercy is offered to all who seek him.

And that is the challenge of the resurrection. Again,

quoting the letter to the Colossians: "If then you were raised with Christ, seek what is above, where Christ is seated at the right hand of God. Think of what is above, not of what is on earth." (Col. 3:1-2) If we want to live new life with Christ in eternity, we must live his new life now.

Hopefully, our Easter celebration will inspire us to leave today with a new resolve to praise the Lord (this is what "Alleluia" means) and to rejoice and be glad because this is the day the Lord has made; this is the day that is a source of hope and salvation for us. Amen.

Second Sunday of Easter
April 19, 2009

INTRODUCTION – (Acts 4:32-35; 1 John 5:1-6; John 20:19-31) I've asked you to greet one another as Mass began in order to create a sense of community. This is an important theme in today's Scriptures. People often ask me, for example: "who is that person who sits in such and such a place at the 10:00 Mass." We have great people in our parish but most people do not know it. They just know a few close friends perhaps. It would be so easy when you are on the way to church or after Mass to just go up to someone you don't know, put out your hand and say: "hello, I'm so and so. What's your name?" If you forget it the next time you see them ask again. I do it all the time. The theme of community is expressed in today's first reading by the care the early Christians had for one another. Unfortunately, this idyllic moment for the early Church did not last. There were those who tried to cheat on the system of sharing their possessions in common, there were defections from the community when persecutions came, there were heresies and there were those who broke away and began a church of their own. The unity Jesus prayed for so earnestly at the Last Supper was short-lived.

HOMILY – We heard about the early Christians' love for one another. How they loved one another was one of the big attractions of the early Church. In today's gospel, there is another very clear picture of how important community is. The apostles were gathered together on Easter Sunday night when Jesus appeared to them. But Thomas wasn't with them. We're not told why. Maybe he was daring enough to go out for food and supplies while the others huddled together in fear that the Roman soldiers or the Jewish religious leaders might come to get them next, maybe he was depressed and wanted to be left alone, maybe he just went out for a walk. For whatever reason Thomas missed getting to see Jesus. He was absent from the community. While all the other apostles as well as the women who had seen Jesus earlier in the day were excited about the resurrection, he must have had a miserable week. It's interesting that it wasn't until a week later when Jesus showed himself again. This second appearance is likely an indication, perhaps inspired by Jesus himself, that, from the beginning, the first day of the week was to be the day for the Christian assembly to gather together to celebrate and to participate in Jesus' saving death and resurrection.

When Thomas was with the others Jesus appeared again. Thomas came to believe. This event shows us how hard it is to believe sometimes, and it also shows us how gathering with the faith community can help our own faith. We don't know whether Thomas actually felt Jesus' hands and side, but Thomas' mind and heart moved beyond mere physical recognition to the most explicit profession of faith in Christ to be found in the Scriptures: "My lord and my God." It is an expression we were taught to say to ourselves when the priest held up the host and the chalice at the consecration. I still say it in my mind. I wonder how many other people do.

Even the forgiveness of sins, a spiritual power which Christ entrusted to his apostles and which we hear about in today's gospel, when it was officially administered sacramentally, was, originally, administered not privately, but was expressed as a reconciliation with the community. People who had sinned seriously were, in effect, excommunicated; they could not participate in the Mass or Communion and they had to do penance before they could officially rejoin the community. That's the way the sacrament of reconciliation was performed in the first few hundred years of the Church's history.

St. Paul tells us people who think they don't need the Church are like a part of the body that says I don't need the rest of the body. We need to be part of a faith community to be nourished spiritually. Jesus promised he would be with us when two or three are gathered together in his name. As he tells us in John 6, we especially need to meet him weekly in the Eucharist to be taught by him in the Scriptures and to be fed by his body and blood without which there is no life in us.

May our gathering together today help us experience his peace, recognize him in faith, unite us with him in love, and deepen our love for one another. Amen.

Third Sunday of Easter
April 26, 2009

INTRODUCTION – (Acts 3:13-15, 17-19; 1 John 2:1-5a; Luke 24:35-48) We take so many of our blessings for granted until, God forbid, we lose one. Take for example the ability to walk. We injure a knee or some part wears out and we find it painful or impossible to do many of the things we just took for granted. What if we were lame from birth and could never join in other kids' games because we couldn't run or walk. There used to be a sick joke about a kid like that who wanted to be on the local baseball team, so his buddies let him play and they used him for third base!

A very short time after Jesus' ascension Peter and John were on their way to the Temple to pray. There was a lame man sitting at the Temple entrance. In that culture, it was bad enough to be handicapped, but a person like that was looked down upon because it was everyone's belief that he must have been a great sinner and he was suffering for his sins. The lame man asked Peter and John for a little money as they passed. Peter said, "I don't have any money, but I will give you what I have. In the name of Jesus Christ of Nazareth, get up and walk." Then Peter helped him to his feet and he was healed. He was so excited, he jumped and danced and praised God. Of course, this created quite a commotion and everyone wondered what had happed. Peter took the opportunity to explain. He credits it all to Jesus. Today's first reading is part of his explanation.

HOMILY – I'm sure most of us have had wonderful life-changing events we could talk about, getting a good job; meeting a wonderful person who changed our life, whether it was a teacher, a friend, or someone who eventually became our spouse; the birth of a dearly loved son or daughter; inheriting a large sum of money; finding a cure for a chronic illness. The lame man I talked about in my introduction, whose healing is described in the third chapter of the Acts of the Apostles, certainly had his life changed dramatically by this encounter with Peter and John.

Today we hear again about the Resurrection of Jesus. Easter is too big a feast to celebrate just one day. We celebrate it for fifty days, and then we continue to celebrate it every Sunday when we gather in faith to meet our risen Lord in the Eucharist. Our gospel today takes us back to Easter Sunday. In the afternoon of Easter Sunday, Jesus appeared to two of his disciples. They were walking away from Jerusalem, discouraged and depressed over Jesus' death. Jesus walked with them, talked to them about the Scriptures, and when he broke bread with them they recognized him. They came running back to the upper room to tell the others. When they got there, they were told Jesus had appeared to Peter and then suddenly Jesus appeared to all of them. In spite of the appearances in the early morning to the women, to the two disciples, and to Peter, Luke tells us the apostles were "terribly frightened." I suppose that would be a normal reaction. Jesus assured them he was very much alive and very well. They could see him and touch him. To give them further proof, he asked for something to eat. He ate something they themselves had prepared to convince them he was real and that they weren't seeing a ghost or seeing him was something out of their own imagination. I have to pause here to tell you something cute. I've told this before so pardon me for repeating it: A mother proudly told her pastor: "My teenage son has finally learned one bible verse. It's Luke 24, verse 41 where Jesus says to his disciples: 'Do you have anything here to eat?'"

Whatever wonderful life-changing events we might think of, the Resurrection of Jesus is the most wonderful life-changing event ever. Because Jesus rose from the dead, our world is a different world. Because Jesus rose from the dead, evil and hatred and suffering have been overpowered. They still hang around inflicting difficulties on us, but their power has been broken by the glory of the Resurrection. Because Jesus rose from the dead, death no longer has the last word over any of us. Death has been overcome by life, eternal life. Even sin will not win out, but forgiveness in Jesus' name will destroy sin. Sin and evil will keep on trying to pull us down and destroy us, but in Christ we are raised up. We must be careful not to give in to sin's destructiveness, John tells us in today's second reading, and the way not to give in is to keep his commandments so his love can be perfected in us. Because Jesus rose from the dead, even fear cannot hold on to us for long, for Jesus came to us offering us peace. Notice that Jesus' first word to the apostles was "peace." Our world is a totally different world now after Jesus' Resurrection. But if it continues to look the same to all of us, with evil and hatred and suffering, maybe we who have been changed by the resurrection are not doing what Jesus said to do. We heard him say at the end of today's gospel: "you are witnesses of these things." This world-changing event has happened and we hope to share in its blessings. It partly depends on us, however, to bring those blessings to the world around us through the witness of our lives, our goodness, our love, our peace and our joy. Let's pause for a moment to ask ourselves how we can witness more fully the Resurrection. Amen.

Fourth Sunday of Easter

May 3, 2009

INTRODUCTION – Last week I spoke about how Peter and John healed a crippled beggar in the Temple. The healed man jumped up and down and was walking around which caused a great amount of commotion in the Temple. The people wanted to know what happened and how it had happened. Peter gave all the credit to

Jesus who, in his risen presence, healed the man through the Apostles. When the Jewish religious leaders, many of whom did not believe in any kind of resurrection, heard Peter's witness, they arrested Peter and John and took them to court. Today we hear a portion of Peter's testimony. The important thing to notice is not only what Peter had to say about Jesus but also his boldness. The court didn't know what to do with Peter and John because all the people were excited about the healing of a man who had been lame for over 40 years. So the court warned the Apostles not to talk about Jesus any more. The Apostles would not be intimidated, however, for they were now filled with the Holy Spirit. (Acts 4:8-12)

HOMILY – Jesus tells us: "I am the good shepherd." Today is often called Good Shepherd Sunday because every year on the fourth Sunday of Easter, we hear a passage from St. John's 10th chapter (Jn. 10:11-18) which is about Jesus as our shepherd.

Today Jesus tells us about two kinds of shepherds. There is the kind of shepherd who owns his or her own sheep and there are shepherds who are hired by a farmer to protect and care for sheep that belong to someone else. The second kind, the hired shepherds, run away when danger comes, while those who own their sheep fight hard to protect what is their own, sometimes getting hurt badly or even getting killed. Jesus is telling us he would be killed to protect and save us, but he would return to life again – which he did. This shows us, first of all, how much he cares for us. He would fight to the bitter end for us. It also shows us how powerful he is that he can lay down his life and take it up again. Peter tells us in today's second reading that Jesus is the only one we can safely follow in order to be saved,.

Jesus tells us something else about shepherds today - they know their sheep and the sheep know their shepherds. It's just the same way we know our pets at home. How do they know one another so well – because they spend a lot of time together. Sheep take a lot of care and the shepherd is with his or her sheep 24 hours a day, seven days a week. Jesus is with us all the time and knows us better than we know ourselves (all the hairs on our heads are numbered – do any of us know ourselves that well?) If we don't know him very well, we need to spend more time with him; and that's called prayer.

When I think of shepherds, I always remember 20 years ago when I climbed Mt. Sinai (I'm glad I did it then, because I couldn't do it any more – it's very rugged and steep) and on the way down, I saw a shepherd and her sheep on a near-by hill. It was just getting dark. She started playing her flute and headed in a direction away from where we were; the sheep just fell in line following her. It was all the sheep trusted her knew how much they depended on her. It was a beautiful scene.

The metaphor is obvious. Christ is our shepherd. He wants us to trust him and follow him. Sometimes following him can get a little frightening; we don't know where he's taking us or what he might ask of us. Sometimes when he takes us through the desert, as shepherds need to do at times when they want to bring their sheep to better grazing ground, we ask why is he doing this to us? That's why he is always telling us we need to have faith in him. That's also why we need to pray - so we will have faith in him. Amen.

Fifth Sunday of Easter
May 10, 2009

INTRODUCTION – (Acts 9:26-31; 1 John 3:18-24; John 15:1-8) Many of the Jews, because they were under Roman occupation, had two names - a Roman name and a Jewish name. Thus Paul also had the name Saul. Most of the time he is called Paul, but occasionally, as in today's first reading, he is called Saul. You remember he was a zealous Pharisee and a fierce persecutor of all who believed in Christ. On one occasion, as he was on his way to Damascus to search out Christians and arrest them, Jesus appeared to him. He immediately discovered Christians had it right and what he was doing was entirely wrong. His life turned around completely and he began preaching and teaching about Jesus. Even after three years in and around Damascus, preaching that Jesus was the Son of God, the Christian community in Jerusalem was not convinced that he was for real. When he first showed up in Jerusalem, the disciples were afraid to trust him. Barnabas was a disciple they did trust and he testified that Paul was genuine. The Hellenists, in the first reading, were Greek speaking Jews who saw Paul as a traitor to Judaism.

HOMILY – Happy Mothers' Day to all our mothers. Friday we had May crowning and so the statue of Mary is still here to remind us of Mary, our spiritual mother, today too. On a Mother's Day card, a six year-old girl wrote her Mother: "Dear Mom, I'm going to make lunch for you on Mother's day. It's going to be a surprise. P.S. I hope you like pizza and popcorn."

In a recent comic strip, For Better or For Worse, Elly, a young mom, had a horrible day caring for her two toddlers who were sick. Looking for sympathy, Elly called her own mother looking for an understanding ear. She told her mom what a horrible 24 hours she had, getting up every half hour during the night and caring for her toddlers all day – first one, then the other. She said to her mom "you don't even get a chance to think about yourself." Then she added I guess you went through all this with me and my brother, didn't you?" There was a pause, then Elly said to her mom, "Er, Mom, did we ever thank you?" "Thanks" is in order constantly, but especially today. Thank you mothers for your love and unselfish dedication and patience. Without you the world would come to a screeching halt.

Jesus is telling us today, without him, all of our lives would go nowhere. He tells us: "Without me you can do nothing. Anyone who does not remain in me will be thrown out like a branch and wither." When we grow up and leave home, our love and our connection with our parents may remain with us, but we are really on our own. It can never be that way with Jesus. We need our Lord when we're 60 or 70 as much as when we're 6 or 7. We need him all the time. If we reflect deeply, we know there is a power greater than ourselves that we depend on and that we constantly need to sustain us. We are connected with that power through Jesus, the true vine.

The prophets, hundreds of years before Christ, used the vineyard as an image of Israel. Just as a farmer would cultivate his vineyard and care for it and expect to harvest grapes from it, so God would care for his people and expect good works from them: devout worship, obedience to his commandments, justice and love for the poor and vulnerable. Jesus is telling us today that through our union with him we are God's people.

Jesus has tried to tell us that in many ways. I would like to mention just five statements where Jesus uses metaphors that tell us how important it is that we remain united with him. Notice each of these begins with the words: "I am." Last Sunday we heard him tell us "I am the good shepherd." "I am the light of the world." "I am the bread of life." "I am the resurrection and the life." And the fifth one we heard today: "I am the true vine." If we had time we could reflect upon how vital each of these items is: shepherds for sheep, light and food for us, the vine for one of its branches. Since vine and branches is the theme of today's gospel, let us stay with that image for just another few minutes.

Quite simply, a vine is an organic structure that is nurtured by the rain and the sun; it is fed by the sap that flows through the stem and the branches; it grows and produces fruit. Jesus tells us he is the true vine, drawing life from the Father and communicating that life to all those who remain united with him. In other words there is a mysterious, living connection between each of us and Christ and a mysterious and living connection uniting us with one another through our union with Christ.

St. Paul used a similar metaphor when he wrote that we are the body of Christ. He tells us Christ is head of the body and we are the members. We are feet, hands, arms, legs, etc. through whom Christ lives in the world today. We are united with Christ and with each other through the Spirit. Pope Pius XII wrote an encyclical called the Mystical Body of Christ describing this union. This is not a connection we can examine under a microscope or test for in any other way, other than the test Jesus gave us when he said "by their fruits you will know them." The way we live our lives shows whether we live in Christ or not.

Sixth Sunday of Easter
May 17, 2009

INTRODUCTION – The issue in today's first reading (Acts 10:25-26, 34-35, 44-48) is how the Apostles (who were Jews) should deal with Gentiles (who were pagans) when these Gentiles came to believe in Jesus. The Apostles believed God revealed his law to Moses. Shouldn't pagan converts to Jesus be required to also follow all that was in the Jewish law: circumcision, strict dietary laws, special feast days, etc.?

St. Peter, the leader of the community, received the answer to this question in a most unusual way. While Peter was in prayer, God gave Peter a vision of many different birds and animals. Many of them were birds and animals the Jews were not allowed to eat, such as pork, shrimp, clams, oysters and many other creatures. (Lev. 11:1-23) God told Peter to eat them. Peter said he would never eat anything forbidden. God said to him: "What God has made clean, you are not to call unclean." God said this three times to Peter. When the vision disappeared, God told Peter there were some men coming to see him and he was to go with them to the home of a Gentile named Cornelius, a high officer in the Roman army. A strict Jew was not allowed to enter a Gentile's house, but God told him to, so he did. When Peter got there he spoke to Cornelius and his relatives and friends about Jesus. As Peter finished speaking, Cornelius and all who were with him were filled with the Holy Spirit. This event is the background for today's first reading. Peter's entire speech is not included in the reading. The liturgy wants to get right to the point - that God's love in Jesus is meant for all people. Peter had finally understood what God had told him in his vision, and without requiring these pagans to be circumcised or requiring them to accept Jewish traditions and customs, he gave the order that they should be baptized.

HOMILY – (2nd Reading: 1 Jn 4:7-10; Gospel: Jn 15:9-17) Probably for most people it may seem like we celebrated Easter two months ago. But the Church continues to celebrate it. Our daily Masses and prayers all reflect an Easter theme and they are filled with Alleluia's. Liturgically it's a beautiful time of the year. We will celebrate Easter for two more weeks.

Every Easter I can't help wondering why Jesus offers us a share in his risen life, why God wants us to live with him forever. Why doesn't God just forget us? In this immense universe God created, we are so small. Why should God go to all the trouble he did to bring us eternal life? Maybe we've never asked ourselves these questions. Maybe we think we are such charming, wonderful creatures that God can't help loving us. Well, we know we humans are not always such wonderful, charming individuals, but it is true that God can't help loving us because that's the way God is. God is love St. John tells us in today's second reading. Just like the sun has to shine because that's what the sun does, God loves us because that's what God does. Yet in spite of our imperfections, God's love reaches out to all people. This was the big revelation we heard about in today's first reading. The Jews presumed they had a monopoly on God's love. Indeed, they did have a monopoly in that God gave them the special gift of his revelation before the time of Jesus, but Jesus fulfilled all that had gone before and revealed that God is calling all people to know his saving love.

We need to know that even though God can't help loving us, because God is love, we will never know the joy he wants to share with us, unless we follow the path he has marked out for us. In today's gospel he tells us, "I have told you this so that my joy may be in you and your joy might be complete." But just like the clouds can block the light of the sun, our sins, our indifference, our neglect can get in the way of God's love that is there for us. He has told us what we need to do. He summed it up in his new commandment: "Love one another as I love you." This is called a new commandment because previously he told us to love our neighbor as ourselves. That's possible for any of us to do, but being able to love as Jesus does, to "love one another as I have loved you," that's really asking a lot. Jesus is God. Can we love like God does? We can, but only with the help of his Holy Spirit who dwells in us and who seeks to transform us into being like Christ.

One of the ways he has loved us is that he laid down his life for us. Can we do that for someone? Many people do. We read about heroes all the time who have risked their lives for someone else. There are people who have dedicated their lives to a job or a vocation where they are less interested in getting rich than they are in doing good for others. I asked the school children in our upper grades yesterday "who would be willing to give up their life for another person?" Only one girl raised her hand. When I asked them if you saw a friend crossing the street and there was a car coming they didn't see it, would you risk your life to run into the street to push them out of the way? Quite a number would. I think many of us are more Christ-like than we imagine ourselves to be. I can't help but mention those who sacrifice their time and energy to serve those who are the most vulnerable in society - the poor, the aged and the unborn.

We have to know that when Jesus talks about "love" he's not talking about the mating instinct, which is good but which is too often exploited in the media as the only kind of love that has any importance. Jesus is talking about giving of ourselves for the benefit of another as he did for us. When he talks about "love," he's not just talking about warm fuzzy feelings, which come and go, but he is talking about a dedication and commitment to serve God and others. When he's talking about "love," he's not talking about always speaking of love; he's talking about action: "Not everyone who says to me Lord, Lord will enter the kingdom of heaven, but only the one who does the will of my heavenly father." Words are important and I think married couples should tell each other they love each other and they should do it all the time, but love is more than words.

Love is the key to everything: it explains why God created us, it explains why Jesus came to earth, it explains why God wants us to live with him forever, it explains the Mass we celebrate, and it explains how we are to act toward one another. Amen.

Feast of the Ascension

May 24, 2009

HOMILY – (Acts 1:1-11; Eph 1:17-23; Mark 16:15-20) In our first reading from the Acts of the Apostles, St. Luke gives us a very graphic, easy to picture description of the ascension of our Lord. But he can't describe to our satisfaction what happened to Jesus after "a cloud took him from their sight." The cloud tells us there is much more to the ascension than we can comprehend right now. The world of God will always be mysterious to us until we get to experience it ourselves. To the extent that they can, the letters of Paul and of others in the New Testament make many attempts to describe theologically what lies beyond that cloud. For example, today's second reading tells us Jesus' ascension took him "far above every principality, authority, power and dominion and every name that is named not only in this age but also in the one to come." In other words, he is greater and more exalted than all of creation. Although he was always Son of God, now, even in his humanity, he is seated at the right hand of the Father in eternal glory. It is a glory that is beyond anything we know at present but hope to share with him someday.

I find it interesting that in the Acts of the Apostles (our first reading) St. Luke tells us Jesus ascended 40 days after Easter, but if we read the conclusion to the gospels of Mark, Luke and John, Jesus is described as ascending to the Father on Easter Sunday. This has always baffled me, but I have tried to reconcile this confusing time element by assuming Jesus' mystical, theological entrance into the glory of the Father happened almost immediately after the resurrection. Jesus, however, made many appearances to the apostles and to others after his resurrection and I think of the ascension 40 days later, as described in today's first reading, as the last of those appearances.

What does any of this have to do with us? How can we apply it to our own spiritual lives? I want to give four suggestions about the ascension that might have some meaning for us.

First of all, we must keep a balanced sense of who Jesus is. Sometimes we may feel very chummy with Jesus. He is our brother, our friend, our daily support, one who is understanding and loving; but he is still so awesome, so greatly exalted. He is Lord and God, he has the authority to tell us how to live and he deserves our adoration and honor. It's fine to feel close and intimate with Jesus and he wants us to; otherwise why would he give himself to us so freely in the Eucharist. We have to balance this closeness with his greatness as our Creator to whom we owe all we have and all we are,

Second, when Jesus' finished the job the Father had given him, he handed that job on to us. One of the last things he said was: "Go, therefore, and make disciples of all nations." Would that we could be half as enthusiastic about our faith as the people who sell products on TV worth $19.99!

Third, even though we can't see his risen body, he is still with us. The last words in Matthew's gospel are: "I am with you always." Of course, the Eucharist gives us the same message each week.

My last point is an inspiration that came to me early this week as I began to meditate on the ascension. It was an idea that kept reoccurring. It seemed as if our Lord was telling me: "be sure to say this about the ascension." Where Jesus has gone is where he wants to bring us. He didn't come to this world just because he was bored with being in heaven and needed something else to do. He came to us and took on our human flesh for only one reason: to take us to himself and to share his life with us. At the Last Supper he told us: "I am going to get a place ready for you and I will come back and take you with me so that where I am you also may be." Our real home is not in this world, as much as we may love our homes. Our home is to be with God. His ascension shows us what he has in mind for us. We say we believe this each week: "I believe in the resurrection of the dead and life everlasting." Today's feast is a lesson about not getting too attached to our present lives. As the letter to the Colossians said on Easter Sunday: "seek the things that are above where Christ is seated at the right hand of the Father."

When life is comfortable for us, we don't like to see things change. That was true of the apostles too. The apostles didn't want Jesus to leave them, but he challenged them to move from a comfortable familiarity with him to a new way to be with him. Sometimes too he challenges us to move into unfamiliar territory, sometimes in little ways and sometimes in major ways. Sometimes events themselves, even tragic and unpleasant ones, disrupt our lives and force us to change. Life never stays the same, but the essentials of our faith continue to anchor us and call us to set our sights on what is ahead for us if we stay united with Christ. Somehow God can draw good out of everything for those who love him. If we stay one with him, we shall one day share his glory. That is our hope, no matter what comes our way.

Pentecost Sunday
May 31, 2009

HOMILY – (Acts 2:1-11; 1 Cor 12:3b-7, 12-13; John 20:19-23) The feast of Pentecost is a very ancient feast that goes back 1000 years before Christ. It was one of the three most important Jewish feasts, and it is one of our three most important feasts. Originally it was a harvest feast. Gradually it came to be a celebration of God giving his Law to the Hebrews at Mt. Sinai and establishing them as his own special people. It was as the Jews were celebrating this feast that the Holy Spirit came upon the first believers in Christ. They were sent forth in power to all people to proclaim God's saving love demonstrated in Jesus' death and resurrection. As I was preparing what I was going to say today, I referred to a book I have, entitled *I Believe in the Holy Spirit* by the Dominican theologian Fr. Yves Congar. The book is almost 700 pages long. It impressed me how much could be said about Pentecost and the Holy Spirit. Just out of curiosity I investigated how often the Holy Spirit was mentioned in the New Testament and I came up with a total of 233 times. I'm not going to try to say it all, so relax! Reading sections of the book, though, makes me realize how fortunate I am that in my job I have the opportunity and the gift to be able to read and reflect on the profound mystery of God and his presence with us in Jesus through the Spirit. (And I receive a salary for doing this! Sometimes I feel guilty taking it for something I enjoy doing so much – but then again there are enough stresses at times that make me think I shouldn't feel guilty about taking a salary.) I am grateful to be a priest and realize that I have been greatly blessed. It just so happens that 45 years ago today I was ordained. My sister Rita, who is also one of my most avid fans, decided to have a memorial card printed for my anniversary with a prayer for priests on the back of the card. I put some on the radiators in case anyone would want one.

I would never have survived as long as I did without the help of God's Holy Spirit. Most of the time I was not even aware that God's Spirit was helping me. It's somewhat like that story of the footprints in the sand. Only as I look back do I see the movement of the Spirit keeping me sane through difficult times, giving me ideas when I couldn't think of the right thing to say, encouraging me when my situation was overwhelming, giving me courage when I was afraid, helping me to pray when my spiritual life seemed to go dry, giving me peace when I lacked it. No wonder Jesus calls the Spirit the "Paraclete," a word which is hard to translate but which means something like: "advocate, mediator, helper, intercessor or comforter."

Many of us probably remember from catechism class naming the fruits of the Spirit and the gifts of the Spirit.

The fruits of the Spirit we hear about in the letter to the Galatians (second reading on Pentecost). They tend to be personal qualities such as love, joy, peace, patience, (kindness, generosity, faithfulness, gentleness, self-control). The gifts of the Spirit include some personal talents but they tend to be more oriented toward building up the community of believers such as the gifts of wisdom, understanding, counsel, fortitude, knowledge, piety, fear of the Lord, as well as the gifts of healing, miracles, prophecy, discernment of spirit, speaking or praying in tongues, interpretation of tongues, teaching, pastoring, and a whole lot of other ways to help us in our ministry to one another. In speaking of the gifts, we cannot forget the greatest of the Spirit's gifts which we often hear about at a wedding. St. Paul tells us the greatest of all the Spirit's gifts is love. St. Augustine, in trying to help us to know for sure whether the Spirit dwells in us, said: "Ask your inner self, if you are full of charity, you have the Spirit of God." (*I Believe in the Holy Spirit*, vol. 2, pg 82)

It's easy to focus on the activity of the Spirit in our personal lives as the Spirit comes to us through prayer and through the sacraments. But as we celebrate Pentecost, we cannot forget on that occasion the Spirit was given to the Church to guide and direct it and to help it to grow. The Spirit came to the Apostles (and perhaps the other 120 members of the early community of believers) not just for their personal enrichment, but to send them out to all people to proclaim God's love shown to us through the death and resurrection of Jesus. It remains our task as Church today, as a community of believers to proclaim God's love. We do this as we gather here in faith right now, but we must also share that love and mystery with others to the extent that we are able.

Jesus encouraged us in St. Luke's gospel to pray for the Spirit when he said: "What father among you would hand his son a snake when he asks for a fish? Or hand him a scorpion when he asks for an egg? If you then, who are wicked, know how to give good gifts to your children, how much more will the Father in heaven give the holy spirit to those who ask him?" (Lk. 11:11-12) Amen.

Trinity Sunday
June 7, 2009

INTRODUCTION – (Deut 4:32-34, 39-40; Rom 8:14-17; Mt 28:16-20) Since history began, humans have honored many gods of many different types (a practice we call polytheism). Only one group of people, the Hebrews, beginning with Abraham, were limited to the worship of one God (a practice we call monotheism). It's only in modern times that people have called into question the existence of God (a practice we call agnosticism or atheism). I am only aware of one exception to the practice of polytheism among all nations and that was a short period in Egypt when the Pharaoh Akhenaten, the father of the famous King Tut, permitted only the worship of the sun god, Aten. This short period of monotheism in Egypt disappeared shortly after Akhenaten's death and his famous son returned things to normal: the veneration of many gods. By the way, Akhenaten lived about 500 years after Abraham, so Akhenaten did not invent monotheism. I have a little story about Abraham that's not in the bible. It's found in Jewish and Islamic literature. When Abraham was a little boy he lived with his parents in Ur (an area in southern Iraq). Abraham's father made statues of the gods people worshipped then – that was the way he made his living and there were lots of gods (over 700 of them) so he must have been kept busy. One day Abraham's father had to go on a business trip and he left Abraham in charge of the shop. Abraham felt disgusted with all those statues of gods and goddesses and broke them all – except for one he left standing in the corner. When his father came home he scolded Abraham for what he had done and little Abraham denied doing it. He pointed to the god standing in the corner and said "He did it." (Kind of a foreshadowing of Abraham's loyalty to one God.) The Assyrians, the Babylonians, the Persians, the Romans, and the Greeks worshipped many gods. The names of some of the Roman gods are still familiar: Mercury, Venus, Mars, Jupiter, Neptune and Pluto. Israel was unique among all the nations in its worship of one God, even though at times they allowed themselves to be seduced by the decadent worship of their pagan neighbors. In today's first reading we hear Moses giving some last minute instructions to God's people before they enter the Promised Land. He tells them there is no other God than the Lord (Yahweh) and that only by being faithful to their God will they prosper. It's still good advice for today's world where polytheism and paganism have been replaced by atheism, hedonism and materialism.

HOMILY – Don Auberger told me last evening that his little niece in the first grade came home after school one day and told her mother she didn't understand the Trinity. They were studying it in school and were going to have a test and she couldn't figure it out. Mother tried to talk to her about faith but she wasn't convinced. She said, "I'm going to look it up on the Internet." I know there's a lot on the Internet, but if someone finds the Trinity explained, would they let me know.

We're dealing with a mystery, a mystery no one can fully understand (at least not in this life – maybe in the next) because it's a mystery of who God is and God is too great for our small minds to fully comprehend. Yet, this is a mystery we cannot casually ignore because it is one of the foundational truths of our faith. Our understanding of Jesus as God's Son and our understanding of the Holy Spirit would be seriously flawed without our belief in the Trinity. If there are still mysteries in our universe, we shouldn't be surprised that God who is greater than all his creations would be mysterious to us. Yet, God wants us to know him and so God continues to reveal God's self to us. The Hebrew people learned from God that there were not many gods but only one, even though all the nations around them for centuries believed differently. When Jesus came, God taught us more about who God is – a lot more.

God revealed his Son whose name was Jesus: a holy man, a great teacher and powerful worker of miracles but most of all one who was brutally executed and rose to life three days later. After his resurrection, Jesus was immediately venerated as Lord and God by his followers. This put the early Christians in a bad place with the Jews, because they were seen by the Jews as polytheists and it put the early Christians in a bad place with the pagans, because the Christians would not worship pagan gods. There were serious struggles among the Christians themselves as to how to explain and verbalize their faith that God is one but Jesus is God and the Father is God (and the Holy Spirit fit in this somehow as well). It would be three hundred years before the language was developed and the concepts clarified that the Church could say Jesus is equal to the Father in every respect and yet distinct from the Father. We profess each week the Creed that formulates this faith: that Jesus is the "only Son of God, eternally begotten of the Father, God from

God, Light from Light, true God from true God, begotten, not made, one in Being with the Father. Through him all things were made." When one takes into account all that was said about Jesus in the Scriptures, no other description of Jesus could logically be accepted or believed. Yet many people were put to death – by Jews, by pagans and by fellow Christians over this belief.

Because it took a little longer to describe how the Spirit fit into this picture, I didn't say much about the Holy Spirit yet. Christians still argue over the Holy Spirit. We, Roman Catholics, claim the Spirit proceeds from the Father and the Son whereas the Greek Church/the Orthodox Church, which is separated from the Holy Father, claims that the Spirit proceeds from the Father through the Son. Some theologians see this issue as the main obstacle to union between the Eastern and Western Churches.

If anything, the mystery of the Trinity communicates that God is a family – a family so closely united that although they are three persons, they are one God. Oneness is not only an important characteristic of God, but God wants us to share that oneness with him and one another (it's what he prayed for with such passion at the Last Supper) and yet we have over 400 different groups who call themselves followers of Christ who can't get along with one another.

Today's mystery is just a peek into who God is, a peek that should inspire us to function more like a family - not a divided family but a united one. This peek into the mystery of God shows us another aspect of this characteristic of unity: God is not sitting alone, God is not needy for a few friends to talk with or to enjoy; the three persons are in such perfect oneness with each other that they are overflowing with love. It is in their overflowing love that God wants us to be part of God's community of love, part of God's family; and here we touch another deep-down mystery: Why would God love us so much to let us share God's life and want to make us part of God's family? In today's celebration of the Eucharist, perhaps we'll understand or experience God's love more fully. Amen.

Body & Blood of Christ

June 1, 1997

HOMILY – (Exodus 24:3-8; Heb 9:11-15; Mark 14:12-16, 22-26) I wonder how many people here have ever seen the Vitamin A in a carrot, the Vitamin C in an orange or the potassium in a banana. I've seen lots of vitamin pills, but I wouldn't know what an actual vitamin molecule looked like even if it came up and bit me. Yet the experts tell us they are in certain foods whether we can see them or not. With this thought in mind we could make a simple comparison with the Eucharist, in so far as we cannot see Christ present in the Eucharist; but it doesn't matter that we can't see him, he is still there. I would like to extend this comparison a bit further. Health experts tell us that without the sufficient amounts of vitamins, minerals, carbohydrates, proteins and fats in our diet we will not be healthy and we may even die. We are told to eat a variety of foods so that we get all the nutrients we need. We tend not to question the health experts that tell us all of this. We trust they know what they are talking about. Even though there is probably no one here who follows their recommendations perfectly, I think many Americans are beginning to pay attention to following a good diet, especially as some of us get older. But there are also many who seem to think that those who promote good nutrition are just trying to take all the fun out of life and so they go their merry way filling themselves full of saturated fats, salt, sugar, nicotine and alcohol. The experts who tell us how to take care of ourselves can't help us much if we don't believe them or follow the suggestions they give us.

Today's feast puts us in touch with another expert, Jesus. He tells us what we need to do to be healthy spiritually. How do we know he is an expert we should listen to. Well, he told us he knows what he is talking about, but he also knows many will not believe him just because he said so. So, he told us if we are not sure we want to believe him, to look at his works. "If I do not perform my Father's works, do not believe me; but if I perform them, even if you do not believe me, believe the works, so that you may realize that the Father is in me and I am in the Father." (Jn 11:37-38) Of course we were not there personally to see the miracles Jesus worked, but there were many who did witness his works and there were those who gave their lives as a testimony that what they preached about Jesus was true. So if we decide to believe the words of those who saw him and knew him and who died for him, then we can only conclude that when he speaks to us about things that are beyond us we ought to listen to what he had to say. And if we listen to what he had to say, we will discover that he has a few things to say about nutrition too. He doesn't tell us about the vitamins and minerals we need to keep our physical lives healthy though. He has a much greater purpose in mind. He tells us, "I came that they may have life and may have it to the full." (Jn 10:10) And the food that will nourish that life is himself. For he tells us "I am the bread of life." (Jn 6:35) "Whoever eats this bread will live forever." (Jn 6:58) Now that's the ultimate healthy diet. Today's gospel tells us how he becomes our food.

If many of us have difficulty trusting and especially if we have difficulty following the research and expertise of those who advocate eating a well balanced and healthy diet, then I suppose it's not too great of a surprise that many have difficulty trusting and especially following the guidance of Jesus who is our expert on eternal life. We see a great number of people, even Catholics, who try to tells us Jesus didn't really mean what he said when he said "This is my body.". They tell us its all symbolism. Long before the Last Supper, many of Jesus' followers walked away from him shaking their heads in disbelief when he said to them "Amen, amen, I say to you, unless you eat the flesh of the Son of Man and drink his blood you do not have life within you." (Jn 6:53) When he saw them walk away, he didn't call them back and say "Heh! Come back, you misunderstood me." He knew they were leaving him because they did understand what he said to them. At that point, he just turned to his apostles and asked "Do you also want to leave?" (Jn 6:67) Jesus is our expert on eternal life and he tells us the food he offers us, which is himself, will nourish us forever. Today's feast challenges our belief in him and in his presence with us in the Eucharist.

There was a time in history when so few people were being fed by the Eucharist that the Church had to make a law saying that Catholics were obliged to receive Communion at least once a year. Even up to 40 or 50 years ago, people went to Communion very seldom. There was a heresy at that time called Jansenism which told people they were unworthy to receive Communion unless they went to confession first. The Eucharist was held in such high respect that people stayed away. Now many people have lost their belief in Christ's presence in the Eucharist, and consequently they stay away too. They stay away in the sense that its too much trouble to come to Mass. It seems to me as if the devil tries every trick he can to keep people away from Communion. Either the devil tells us it is so sacred we shouldn't receive it, or he tells us there's nothing worth going there for anyway.

The real crisis of faith in the Catholic Church at the present time I think has its origin right here in the mystery we celebrate today. There are many who no longer believe that the Eucharist is really and truly the body and blood of Jesus Christ. I think this lack of belief is connected with the vocation crisis. I think it's the reason Mass attendance has dropped off. And then, like a domino effect, when people get away from church and Mass attendance, they are getting away from their spiritual roots. Without a strong spiritual foundation to build our lives on, we are left with fewer values to live by and fewer values to pass on to our children. Do I overemphasize the importance of the Eucharist? I don't think so. Certainly God's love is shown to us in many ways, but I believe the Eucharist helps us to see those ways more clearly in which God's love is present in our lives and I believe it is also the Eucharist itself, more than anything else, that tells us that God loves us and that God is with us.

12th Sunday in Ordinary Time
June 21, 2009

INTRODUCTION – (Job 38:1-8; 2 Cor. 3:14-17; Mk. 4:35-41) We learn from the day we get punished for something we didn't do that: "Life is not fair." This feeling is one of the most common reasons people give up their faith in God. The book of Job was an attempt to understand this dilemma: "How can God be just and fair and still allow bad things to happen to good people." As pointed out several times in the story of Job, he was a righteous man. In spite of his goodness, he suffered all kinds of tragedy, and he wanted to know why. The question of innocent suffering is dealt with in 42 chapters. Our first reading today gives us a tiny, tiny portion of God's answer to Job. Basically God told Job, "You don't know anything about how the universe operates; just let me take care of things and trust me." The encounter with God that Job experienced was enough of an answer that somehow satisfied Job. Perhaps the fact that God answered him, even though Job didn't understand, was all the satisfaction he needed.

HOMILY – All world religions are built on the basic premise that if we do good we will be rewarded and if we do evil we will be punished. It's the basic belief of the Hindu's and Buddhists (the law of Karma – where our next life is determined, for better or for worse by the good or bad things we did in this life), it was the belief of the ancient pagans although pagan gods seemed to be more interested in being given due worship and sacrifice than in moral behavior, it was the belief of the Egyptians, it was the belief of the Jews. Let us listen, for example, to Moses' last words to his people before they entered the promised land. "If you obey the commandments of the Lord, your God, you will live and grow numerous and the Lord your God will bless you in the land you are entering to occupy. If, however, you turn away your hearts and will not listen, I tell you now that you will certainly perish."

I certainly support this theology – a good life will be a blessing for us and an evil life will bring us many problems – in this life and the next. Now the Jews did not have any understanding of the next life as we believe in it. Up until a couple of hundred years B.C. they expected that any reward or punishment a person had coming to them happened in this life. But everyday experience often seems to work the opposite. Good people seem to suffer unfairly, while bad people seem to get by with murder (literally or figuratively).

The book of Job struggled with this problem perhaps some 500 years before Christ. We still struggle with the problem of innocent people suffering. Some pagan religions concluded that their gods were not powerful enough or did not care enough to stop evil in the world; or perhaps they were not petitioning the right gods; similar to this some modern writers concluded that God was dead. Other religions, especially early Christian heretics called Gnostics, held that there are two supreme deities, one good and one evil, and they are constantly in conflict with one another in their efforts to influence the world for good or for evil. Three explanations that we can relate to, although other religions hold these too, are: 1) There is no such thing as a truly "innocent" person. We're all guilty of sin and evil desires even if we do not act on them. The idea of Original Sin helps explain the presence of evil in all of us. We can find this idea in St. Paul's epistle to the Romans. Thus there is no such thing as "innocent" human suffering. There is only God's mercy for the sinner. 2) A second answer to suffering is that suffering is a crucial step in preparing for salvation. Salvation results from lessons we can only learn through suffering, such as humility, or that we are not spiritually self-sufficient, or we must seek God's mercy. 3) Lastly suffering is only temporary, even if it lasts a lifetime in this world. In reality, this life is only a moment compared to eternity.

Whatever explanation or combination of explanations we may choose to accept, for me the final solution to the problem of good people suffering depends on the attitude that we have towards it and the important attitude is trust. St. Paul said "for those who love God, all things work for the best." That's what keeps me optimistic. Trust. It's not much different than the relationship we had with our parents when we were young. We had to take a lot of things on faith until we were old enough to understand. And as we congratulated our mothers a few weeks ago, today we congratulate our fathers, the first people we learned to trust and we thank them for the ways they imparted life to us.

As I conclude I would like us to think of today's gospel for a moment. Whether we were ever caught in a storm on the sea or not, like the Apostles in today's gospel, we've all gone through emotional life experiences that were just as frightening. And we've all had times when we thought Jesus was asleep, when we've prayed and prayed and received no answer; times when we wanted to ask him "do you not care that we are perishing?" What was Jesus' answer? After he calmed the sea he asked: "Why are you terrified? Do you not yet have faith?" Doesn't that say it all? Amen.

Birth of John the Baptist

June 24, 2007

INTRODUCTION – We are mostly familiar with John the Baptist from the readings during Advent, as John was the prophet who immediately preceded Jesus and foretold his coming. His birthday is June 24, which usually falls on a weekday. It is considered an important feast, so important in fact that when it falls on Sunday, it takes precedence over the Sunday readings. For those who like to follow the readings in the red Worship book, they are 1038 (eve) or 1039 (day). If you are curious why the feast of his birth is today, consider this. When the archangel Gabriel appeared to Mary, the archangel told her that her cousin Elizabeth was already in her sixth month. The church figured that John's birth had to have been six months before the birth of Jesus. So, Christmas is six months away.

The liturgy usually puts the feast days of saints on the day they died and entered into eternal life. Only three birthdays are celebrated: John the Baptist, Mary the mother of Jesus and Jesus himself. This is because their birth is considered especially holy since they were born free from any sin.

[at 4:00 (Vigil)] (Jer 1:4-10; Luke 1:5-17)

Our first reading is from Jeremiah, a prophet who lived 600 years before Christ. The reading describes the role of a prophet as was John the Baptist. It is a fitting description of John.

The gospel is the annunciation to John's father, the old priest Zechariah, that he and his elderly wife would have a child, a special child who would prepare God's people for the coming of the Messiah.

[at 8:00 and 10:00] (Isa 49:1-6; Luke 1:57-66, 80)

In today's first reading, the prophet Second Isaiah, who lived about 500 years before Christ, speaks of some mysterious person who was identified simply as God's servant. This poem and three others in Isaiah's writings are known as Servant Songs. The early Church found these songs described Jesus in a most uncanny way. They are usually read during Holy Week. Today, however, the liturgy applies this second of the Servant Songs to John the Baptist because it states: "the Lord called me from birth, from my mother's womb he gave me my name."

When the archangel Gabriel had appeared to John's father Zachariah nine months earlier, he told him his wife Elizabeth would have a son and he was to be named John. Zachariah and Elizabeth were an older couple and Zachariah didn't believe the angel. Not smart! He lost the ability to speak because of his lack of faith. (It's like the angel would not allow him to speak out his doubts but to keep his lack of faith to himself.) We hear in the gospel how Zachariah's ability to speak returned once John was born.

HOMILY – Since I gave a long introduction, I do not have a very long sermon. Or as Henry VIII said to his third wife, "I will not keep you long." One of Aesop's most famous fables is the story of the ant and the grasshopper.

The story goes like this:

In a field one summer's day a Grasshopper was hopping about, chirping and singing to its heart's content. An Ant passed by, bearing along with great toil a kernel of corn he was taking to the nest. "Why not come and chat with me," said the Grasshopper, "instead of toiling and moiling in that way?" "I am helping to lay up food for the winter," said the Ant, "and recommend you to do the same." "Why bother about winter?" said the Grasshopper; we have got plenty of food at present." But the Ant went on its way and continued its toil. When the winter came the Grasshopper had no food and found itself dying of hunger, while it saw the ants distributing every day corn and grain from the stores they had collected in the summer. Then the Grasshopper knew: "It is best to prepare for the days of necessity."

Solid, practical, down to earth wisdom from 2500 years ago! It's still true. If we do not learn this lesson when life is good, we'll regretfully learn it when it's too late. This goes for education, investing, health and all kinds of important areas of life. John the Baptist's role in life was to insist on the need to prepare. He called people to repent and prepare for the coming of God's kingdom. His message is as important today as it ever was. There is a kind of new age theology that follows the attitude of the Grasshopper. It says don't worry. We're all going to heaven. We'll all be happy in the end. God wants all people to be saved, as St. Paul tells us, but there are abundant passages in every part of the Scriptures that warn us that salvation is not a given. There are things that are necessary for salvation and things that will prevent our salvation. The gentle, loving Jesus, who revealed to us so clearly the love of God, warned us: "The door to heaven is narrow. Work hard to get in, because many will try to enter and will not be able." (Luke 13:23) Jesus, too, like John the Baptist called us to repentance and conversion of heart. I think the most important lesson we can learn from this feast of John the Baptist is to prepare. The fact you are here today is one good sign that you understand the need to prepare. If you want some more specific ideas, the insert in today's bulletin about love of God might give you a few good ideas on how to prepare better. Amen.

13th Sunday in Ordinary Time
July 2, 2000

INTRODUCTION – (Wis 1:13-15, 2:23-24; 2 Cor 8: 7, 9, 13-15; Mark 5:21-43) The first reading tells us God did not make death. Rather, it came about through the envy of the devil. This is obviously a commentary on the story of Adam and Eve in the garden – how they tried to find their happiness and fulfillment by doing things their way rather than God's way. They didn't trust what God told them. Often we blame Adam and Eve for all the problems in the world and say if they hadn't sinned we would be in much better shape, but we're no different. Too often we chose not to trust God and seek our happiness and fulfillment by doing things our way rather than doing what God tells us we must do. When the reading tells us that those who belong to the company of the devil experience death, it is referring to spiritual death.

The second reading is an appeal to the Corinthians for financial help for the poor in Jerusalem.

HOMILY – Today is the 13th Sunday of Ordinary Time. Ordinary Time in the Church calendar is all the time of the year that is not included in the Advent/ Christmas cycle or the Lent/Easter cycle. In other words, we will be in Ordinary Time now until December when the season of Advent begins. The color for Ordinary time is green – a symbol of hope.

Hope is the attitude that has to carry all of us through life. We either live a life of hope or we live lives that are hope-less – that is, we live lives of despair. Our readings today remind us of what our hope is built upon. Despite the marvelous discoveries of science, such as we heard a lot about this week with the successful mapping of the human genome – which might help find cures for many diseases - none of us are not going to live in this world forever. I heard a good story told by Charles Colson (of Watergate fame who was put in prison and who had a conversion experience). He told this story at the Catholic Men's Conference held earlier this year. It was about a man who was a workaholic. He got to the point that he was nervous and irritable, had high blood pressure, couldn't sleep and was in general falling apart. He went to see the doctor along with his wife. The doctor told him that he was physically exhausted and he had to get some rest or he wouldn't survive. He prescribed six months away from work and resting at home. The doctor then wanted to talk with the man's wife, alone. He told her her husband was critically ill and she had to be an essential part of his recovery. She had to see that he got all the rest he could, not to argue with him, wait on him as much as possible and make life as peaceful and pleasant as she could. If she didn't her husband was going to die. On the way home the husband asked his wife "What did the doctor want to talk with you about?" She answered him, "The doctor told me you were going to die." Well, that's true of all of us, hopefully not in the near future though. God didn't create us to live in this world forever. He created us to live with him forever in a life that is quite different than this present life.

The Bible teaches over and over again, as we heard in today's first reading, that we create our own unhappiness by refusing to trust – to have faith in what God has spoken to us. Most of all, God has spoken to us through his Son, Jesus Christ. And Jesus himself has clearly told us is the way that leads us into the life God wants to share with us. "I am the way, and the truth and the life."

The most powerful lines in today's Gospel for me are, "do not be afraid, just have faith." These words come right after Jairus is informed that his daughter has died. In spite of appearances, Jesus tells him to keep believing that Jesus could help him. The Gospel is about events that touch all of our lives at one time or another, events that frighten us all: illness for which there is no cure and death, especially the death of a young person. Jesus came to tell us "do not be afraid, just have faith." These lines kept going through my mind this morning as I attended the funeral of a young man who has been very generous to me and my classmate by giving us a place to stay when we go on vacation. The man was younger than I am, so you know he was very young! Jesus is telling us appearances are deceiving. He told Jairus, "Your daughter is asleep." For all who believe in and follow Christ, this is true. Death is only a falling asleep. Jesus is in our midst today, as we gather in prayer, as we hear his word, as we receive his body and blood. Can we reach out to touch him and be open to whatever grace he might give us; can we hear him say, "do not be afraid, just have faith"?

14th Sunday in Ordinary Time

July 5, 2009

INTRODUCTION – (Ezekiel 2:2-5; 2 Cor. 12:7-10; Mark 6:1-6) Sometimes prophets predicted the future, but most of the time their task was to remind God's people of how God wanted them to live. Their efforts to do so were not always appreciated by the people who heard their message. The prophet Ezekiel lived about 600 years before Christ. He had to warn the people of the great destruction that was soon to come if they did not change their ways. We hear in today's first reading God cautioning Ezekiel that as a prophet he would not have an easy job of it. The passage prepares us for the gospel that tells of Jesus, the greatest prophet of all, who was rejected by his own people when he came to preach in his hometown of Nazareth.

HOMILY – At times we all have put people on a pedestal who ended up disappointing us and we've looked down upon people who were much better off than we are. I've done that many times. An example of this came to me as I was reading the newspaper about Bernard Madoff. Madoff swindled thousands of people out of billions of dollars and you may have heard that this week he was sentenced to 150 years in prison. Sometimes there is justice. My point is that at the end of the article there was a statement from his wife who said: "The man who committed this horrible fraud is not the man whom I have known for all these years." Sometimes we think we know someone and we really don't.

In Jesus' case his family, friends and neighbors thought they knew him. In their estimation he was just one of them, a day laborer turned preacher. He didn't belong to the priestly class or have an extensive formal education in Jerusalem like other religious leaders. Maybe a few were impressed, but most couldn't believe he was anyone special, in spite of the stories that were being told about him and the wondrous things he was doing. St. Mark tells us he couldn't do much to help any of them. This is a powerful statement and we find it only in St. Mark: "he was not able to perform any mighty deeds there, apart from curing a few sick people" The message is obvious: a lack of faith actually prevents God from helping us as he would like.

The lesson for us in this gospel is that we have to be careful not to tell ourselves that we know who Jesus is. Oh, we know some things about Jesus. We learned them from our parents, we learned them in school, we learned them in the bible, we learned them in church. We profess our faith in Jesus every Sunday, and so we think we know all about Jesus.

St. John of the Cross, a sixteenth century mystic, would tell us no matter what we know about Jesus, it is hardly just the beginning. He said Jesus "is like a rich mine with many pockets containing treasures: however deep we dig we will never find their end or their limit. Indeed, in every pocket new seams of fresh riches are discovered on all sides."

The people I have met who are convinced they know all they need to know about Jesus are those who know him least. How do we come to know who Jesus is? To build on what we already know, we constantly need prayer, the sacraments (especially the Eucharist) and service to others. We do need all three of these: prayer, sacraments and service to others. Any one of these three alone does not work very well without the other two.

As I preach this I have to confess that for all the theology and scripture I have studied, for all the time I spend in church, I'm not necessarily any better than anyone else in really knowing our Lord. More often than I would like to admit, I say my prayers with not enough attention to what I'm saying, I receive Communion with my mind on a half dozen other things. I just pray that the Lord is merciful to me, because I do try to give him my love and to know him better.

That's part of the reason we are here today, to get to know Jesus better than we already do. Today is Independence Day. Today we celebrate our freedom. More and more it seems to me today's culture believes freedom means doing whatever you want. More and more our citizens seem to think freedom means freedom from God and what God wants us to do or not do. We see it in statistics of how people are taking their religion less and less seriously. If you want to do something for our Country, start inviting a friend who does not come to church much to come to Mass with you. Maybe they will discover God's love more deeply. I hope you all have a great holiday. I hope that as you celebrate today you will pause to be grateful to God, the source of freedom, and to be grateful to those who have gone before us in this life who have entrusted to us the freedom and the blessings we enjoy. Amen.

15th Sunday in Ordinary Time
July 12, 2009

INTRODUCTION – (Amos 7:12-15; Eph 1:3-14; Mark 6:7-13) Last week, in reference to the prophet Ezekiel, I commented that sometimes prophets predicted the future but most of the time they tried to direct God's people to live by God's laws. Consequently, they were not usually appreciated. Today, in our first reading, we hear from the prophet Amos who lived over 700 years before Christ. In that culture were professional prophets who made a nice living from telling people how to solve their problems, giving them advice, predicting the future, etc. Usually these professionals did not speak for God, rather they spoke the kinds of things their clients would be pleased with hearing. If they offered any criticism or anything offensive they would not have been paid their fee. When Amos went to Bethel, a place of worship in the north, which was established in competition with the true Temple in Jerusalem, Amos did not have warm fuzzy things to say about the way God's people were living. The high priest, Amaziah, mistook him for one of the professional prophets and told him to go back home and prophesy. Amos protested that he was not a career prophet, rather he was living a nice peaceful life as a farmer and God called him to go to Bethel and warn the people that their sinful lives would lead to destruction. Today's passage prepares the way for the gospel where Jesus sends his apostles out to preach and warns them they may not always be welcome.

HOMILY – Amos claimed that he was sent by God to preach. It wasn't something he decided to do on his own, nor did he intend to make himself rich doing it. Because the high priest there had the king and his army on his side, it's most likely that the high priest succeeded in throwing Amos out of town. The job of telling people they need to repent is about as much fun as telling people to cut off their right hand. It seldom happens. John the Baptist had some success in preaching repentance, but we all know how he was eventually beheaded. St. Mark tells us in today's gospel how Jesus sent the Twelve out to preach repentance, to cast out demons, and to heal the sick. It's from the fact that they had been sent out that they get the title of apostle. That's what the Greek word "apostolos" means, one who has been sent out.

Like a mother bird teaching its little ones to fly, Jesus was giving his apostles their first lessons in the work they would later do when he was no longer with them in physical form. In doing God's work, Jesus was obviously insisting they learn to trust in God for what they needed. He instructed them to bring nothing with them except the clothes they were wearing. Jesus seems to stress their living a simple life style almost as much as he stresses the message they are to bring. My suspicion too is that the apostles were probably going to be away for a short period of time. If they had to be gone for months, they would have needed a few more things. For example, when Paul was traveling, he had to bring books and the tools of his trade as a tent maker and enough clothes because it was bitterly cold in the areas where he evangelized.

I wonder whether the idea Jesus had of the apostles not taking too much stuff along when they went out to preach might also apply to how many ideas a person should try to stuff into a homily. I was on retreat last week and I had all week to think about this gospel. I had lots of things I wanted to say. When I was putting my homily together, I had hoped to say something about the priesthood, since this year has been proclaimed by the Holy Father as the year of the priest. When I started putting all my thoughts on paper, it left little room to say much about priests. I do want to say, however, I feel very strongly that I've had a call and have been sent out. It is very gratifying when I discover something I've said or done has brought a person closer to God. But sometimes there is rejection as well. It's a delicate thing to know what to say when you want to lead a person to do the right thing. I don't want to face God who might say to me, "you should have said something," and at the same time I don't want to alienate a person totally. That is one of the hardest things about being a priest. I'm sure many of you parents and grandparents face the same dilemma. As I said earlier, asking someone to stop doing something they shouldn't or to start doing something they should is at times like asking them to cut off their right hand. In this year of priests, I hope you will remember to pray for priests. There is an insert in today's bulletin about the priesthood, so you can read more about it if you choose.

There is one last point I want to make. Jesus' apostles were sent to heal the sick who they anointed with oil. Mark's gospel and the Letter of James give us the basis for the sacrament of the sick. There are people, some saints for example, who have a special gift of healing, but the sacrament of the sick has a special power in and of itself, independent of the holiness of the priest. We've not offered the sacrament lately, so if anyone would like to receive it after Mass today, I will be available. Amen

16th Sunday in Ordinary Time
July 19, 2009

HOMILY – (Jeremiah 23:1-6; Eph 2:13-18; Mark 6:30-34) There was a man who worked in a museum whose job it was to explain the different exhibits. On one occasion he pointed to the bones of a dinosaur saying the bones were 100 million and 9 years old. Someone asked how they could date those bones so accurately. He said "well, when I started working here, I was told these bones were 100 million years old and I've worked here for nine years."

Today I want to give everyone a little history lesson. I'm not going back to the dinosaurs, but I am going back pretty far – to King David, 1000 years before Christ. When I was in school, I hated history. It wasn't until we studied the history of the Old Testament in the seminary that I began to appreciate it. I cannot cram 1000 years of history into a couple of minutes. I just want to touch on the parts of Jewish history that are mentioned in today's reading. If you want to learn more, read everything in the Old Testament, but be sure you have a commentary to help you. Otherwise, you'll give up in despair because you won't know what it's all about - especially the prophets and the historical books.

When David was king 1000 years before Christ, David wanted to build a house for God, since there was no Temple for God at that time. God did not give David permission to do so, however God promised David through the prophet Nathan that he would bless him and build David a house in the sense that David's kingdom would continue forever and one of his descendants would always rule. This blessing lasted through the reign of David's son, Solomon; but we humans somehow have the ability to sabotage God's blessings. Solomon turned to pagan gods and over-extended the country financially by elaborate building projects and exorbitant taxes, so when Solomon died there was a rebellion and most of Israel broke away from Solomon's successor, David's grandson, Rehoboam. Rehoboam continued to rule over the southern part of Israel, the area we know as Judaea . For 400 years (and this is amazing) the kings of Judaea were descendants of King David. The northern kingdom that rebelled against David's successors suffered under a succession of kings and rebellions. In less than 300 years the northern kingdom was destroyed by the Assyrians, people from northern Iraq. About 100 years after that, the Babylonians from southern Iraq conquered the Assyrians and took control of the entire Middle East. The conquest of the Babylonians brings us up to Jeremiah whom we heard in today's first reading. At the time of Jeremiah, here was the situation: the northern kingdom no longer existed. The southern kingdom, Judaea, was still being ruled by David's descendants but they were not loyal to God or to God's laws. Jeremiah spoke to these kings as they came into power, the last four being: Jehoahaz, Jehoiakim, Jehoikin and Zedekiah. Zedikiah, the last reigning king, died in disgrace. After the Babylonians captured him, his sons were slaughtered before his eyes, he was then blinded and led off to Babylon in chains where he presumably died. You can read how Jeremiah spoke with them in great detail in the book of Jeremiah. He told them exactly what they needed to do to survive the invading forces of Babylon. His messages were ignored. He blames them and their leadership for the destruction that came upon God's people. As we heard in today's first reading, God speaks through Jeremiah: "Woe to the shepherds who mislead and scatter the flock of my pasture." God said he would take over shepherding his people; he would bring them back from exile; he would appoint leaders over them who would serve them well and lead them to peace and security. It took 600 years before God thought the world was ready for this king who would reign and govern wisely, who would do what is just and right in the land.

But then he came, through the announcement of an

angel to a virgin who was engaged to a man named Joseph of the house of David, and the virgin's name was Mary. And the angel said to her "Do not be afraid Mary, for you have found favor with God. Behold, you will conceive in your womb and bear a son, and you shall name him Jesus. He will be great and will be called Son of the Most High, and the Lord God will give him the throne of David his father, and he will rule over the house of Jacob forever, and of his Kingdom there will be no end."

In last week's gospel, Jesus sent his apostles out to heal and cast out demons and to call people to repentance. In today's gospel we are told of their return, excited over their experience and tired. Jesus wanted to some time off, but he couldn't. The mission of Jesus and his apostles apparently was so successful that a great crowd caught up with them before they had chance to catch their breath. Mark describes Jesus taking compassion on them (his heart was moved with deep sympathy for them would probably be a better translation). He saw them as sheep without a shepherd, - people without leadership, and he began to teach them.

One of the important messages in today's readings is that in love our Lord leads us, by teaching us and appointing others to teach us. But we need to listen, and we need to keep on listening. We'll never be finished listening and learning as long as our world suffers from injustice, poverty, hunger, discrimination, war, hatred and killing of innocent people. Christ would be put to death before he would stop teaching. It is to our own great loss when we stop listening. That's one of the reasons we are here each weekend, to listen and to learn. We call ourselves disciples. The word disciple means learner. When we've quit learning, we've quit being a disciple.

17th Sunday in Ordinary Time
July 26, 2009

HOMILY – (2 Kings 4:42-44; Eph 4:1-6; John 6:1-15) We have been reading from St. Mark's gospel this year. In our gospel last Sunday, Mark told us about Jesus and the apostles needing to get away after a period of intense ministry. They got in a boat to go to a deserted area where they could rest awhile. However, the people figured out where they were going and got there ahead of them. Jesus, moved with compassion, realized their need for leadership and responded to the crowd by teaching them.

Then the disciples notice the day is getting late and the people need to eat, so they ask Jesus to send the people away so they can buy some food at nearby farms and villages. Jesus told the disciples to go ahead and feed the people. The apostles protest that would be impossible. Jesus asks how much food they have. Without mentioning a young boy, the apostles report they have five loaves and two fish. With these Jesus feeds 5000. Matthew gives us the detail that it was 5000 men, plus all the women and children. Incidentally, this is the only miracle of Jesus (other than the resurrection) that is recorded in all four gospels (and Matthew and Mark tell us about Jesus feeding a great crowd miraculously a second time). It must have been an awesome event to have been spoken of six times in the gospels. The first three gospels only hint at the Eucharistic implications of this miracle, but John elaborates on it at length. The lectionary switches over to St. John's gospel (the 6th chapter) at this point. I love St. John best among all the gospels and this is one of my favorite chapters in St. John. We'll be reading from this chapter in John until the end of August when we will go back again to St. Mark.

John has a few interesting details that differ from the other gospels. John tells us Jesus and the apostles had already arrived at the place where Jesus fed the people and the people followed him there. It's easy to imagine that some people did arrive before Jesus did and many others came afterwards.

Another detail is that in John Jesus had already anticipated feeding the people when he saw them coming to him. He didn't need to be advised by the apostles that the people might be hungry. He knew in his heart what he was going to do. In John's gospel Jesus is always in control of the situation.

The detail about the boy who was willing to share his small meal (five loaves and two fish) is a beautiful image – as well as a meaningful one. John alone tells us it was barley loaves. This was the bread that the poor ate. This detail shows us the importance of sharing. In today's world God continues to feed six billion people with enough food, but we're not doing very good in sharing what we have. For all kinds of reasons, many people suffer starvation while many others suffer from diseases triggered by having too much to eat. I think the image of the boy who shared his small meal is also an image that whatever we are willing to give to God will come back to us many times over. It took trust on the part of the boy to share the little he had. It takes trust to give over to God the little we feel we have to offer in terms of time, talent or treasure, but it works. God can do a lot with the little we are willing to give.

John tells us Jesus gave thanks over the loaves and fish. I might point out that the Greek verb to give thanks is "eucharisteo." Right from the beginning of chapter six, John links the feeding of the multitude with the eucharist. The eucharistic theme is also hinted at in the command of Jesus, given in all the gospels, to gather the fragments together. Notice in the gathering of fragments it only mentions the loaves. The fish are no longer an important item.

There are twelve baskets left over, not a coincidence that there are twelve apostles. Symbolically they would be the ones to take the bread of life to the world.

One important word here is the word "sign." John does not call it a miracle, but a "sign" which means what Jesus did points to something else. Picture a world without signs. It would be impossible to picture. Signs are what we use to communicate: from body language, to street signs, to words themselves. God speaks to us through signs too. Many of us perhaps remember the definition of a sacrament: "an outward sign" In the next few weeks, we will learn in depth what Jesus was telling the crowd and was telling us in this sign. Amen

18th Sunday in Ordinary Time

August 2, 2009

INTRODUCTION – (Ex 16:2-4, 12-15; Eph 4:17, 20-24; John 6:24-35) The first reading tells us God did not make death. Rather, it came about through the envy of the devil. This is obviously a commentary on the story of Adam and Eve in the garden – how they tried to find their happiness and fulfillment by doing things their way rather than God's way. They didn't trust what God told them. Often we blame Adam and Eve for all the problems in the world and say if they hadn't sinned we would be in much better shape, but we're no different. Too often we chose not to trust God and seek our happiness and fulfillment by doing things our way rather than doing what God tells us we must do. When the reading tells us that those who belong to the company of the devil experience death, it is referring to spiritual death.

The first reading gives us some background for the gospel. It tells how God fed his people with manna 1300 years earlier as Moses led them through the desert to the promised land. In their conversation with Jesus in the gospel, the people refer to this event from the Book of Exodus.

HOMILY – Last Sunday we heard how Jesus fed a great crowd in a miraculous way and how the people wanted to make him a king. Today's gospel is something of a surprise in that we hear how the crowd challenged him to give them a sign in order for them to believe in him. They believed in him enough to want him for their king, but now they seem to take a different attitude toward Jesus. It doesn't seem to make sense. We know crowd's can be erratic and fickle, but I think there's more to the story than this.

What I think is going on here is that Jesus wanted the people to take him on his terms while the people were willing to take Jesus on their terms but not on his. I will explain. The people were approaching Jesus on a material, worldly level. Jesus said, "you are looking for me not because you saw signs but because you ate the loaves." It wasn't just a free fish dinner they were seeking; they wanted a king to free them from the power of Rome and to establish their independence. Jesus was trying to lift their thinking from a worldly, material level to a more spiritual level. He told them he fed them as a sign that he wanted to feed them with bread that comes from heaven, from God himself, bread that would nourish them for eternal life. But Jesus said they didn't see the meaning of the sign that he had worked. There was much more to the sign than a free meal. There was much more to the sign than the possibility that he could be the long awaited king who would restore independence to their nation. We can't be too hard on them for not recognizing the profound meaning of this sign – how could they have figured it out by themselves. They needed Jesus to explain to them the meaning behind what he had done. That's exactly what Jesus planned to do as he continued teaching them.

An important part of his teaching was when he told them not to work for food that perishes but for food that endures for eternal life. Is Jesus saying people do not need to work for the food they need each day and for the other things they need, like clothing and shelter and security? Should we all just sit around and pray or watch TV all day and depend on the government to take care of us? That's not what Jesus is saying. He himself worked at skilled labor for almost all of his life: ("Is not this the carpenter?" they ask in Mark 6:3 when Jesus began his work as a teacher and healer). Even the apostle Paul said to the Thessalonians: "When we were with you, we instructed you, that if anyone was unwilling to work, neither should that one eat." (2 Thes. 3:10). Jesus is not being impractical when he tells us not to work for perishable food. He is being more than practical in that he is telling us this world is not all we have to worry about. He is more than practical in telling us we have to look beyond devoting our time and energy only to our immediate needs. We must also look to the future, not just in this life but also to our eternal future. Fr. Pedro Arrupe, former Superior General of Jesuits throughout the world said: "Nothing is more practical than finding God…What you are in love with, what seized your imagination, will affect everything. It will decide what will get you out of bed in the morning, what you will do with your evenings, how you will spend your weekends, what you read, who you know, what breaks your heart, and what amazes you with joy and gratitude. Fall in love, stay in love, and it will decide everything." (*My Life with the Saints*, James Martin, S.J. pg 119)

The way to that love, that eternal future, that all absorbing preoccupation with the eternal and infinite God, Jesus tells us is himself. When the people ask, "What can we do to accomplish the works of God?" it sounds as if they are looking for some simple task they can do and be done with it. As Jesus tells us, doing the works of God is to believe in the one he sent - Jesus himself. "I am the bread of life; whoever comes to me will never hunger, and whoever believes in me will never thirst." The people begin to see that Jesus is asking for total commitment to himself, so it's not surprising that they ask for another sign. Although Jesus is asking for a lot and he desires to give us a lot, he's asking us to accept him on his terms and not to try to take him and follow him on our terms. Doing the works of God is work because we have to die to ourselves and our own selfishness and live the life he has shown us how to live. A lot of people I know would say it's not hard to believe in Jesus, because they take him on their terms, agree with what they like about him and ignore what they don't like.

Although we might say that believing in Jesus and following him is work, when we do give our lives over to him completely, believing in him and following him comes easier. Until we do give ourselves to him in every way, we will continue to hunger in our hearts and will not know what it is we hunger for; for only he can satisfy us. Amen.

Transfiguration
August 6, 2006

INTRODUCTION – Our first reading is from the book of Daniel (Dn. 7:7-10, 13-14). The author of this book lived during the time the Greeks dominated most of the known world. The Greeks were trying to get everyone to follow their religion (paganism) and any Jew who remained faithful to his or her Jewish faith was put to death. This was the first time in the history of the world that people were persecuted for their beliefs. The book of Daniel tried to offer the Jewish people hope: hope of a savior. This salvation comes from one like a "son of man" whom God endows with kingship and power. Our reading is one of Daniel's visions and it first describes God who is called the Ancient One - indicating God's eternity. The term "son of man" means simply a human being, but this "son of man" would be unique and would be the savior of God's people. This was the favorite title Jesus used in referring to himself. The glory of God is described in today's first reading. It is shown through Christ in his Transfiguration, which is described in today's gospel (Mk. 9:2-10), and in today's second reading from the Second Letter of St. Peter (1:16-19).

HOMILY – Last Sunday I said that for the next four weeks we would be hearing from the sixth chapter of St. John on the Eucharist. I hadn't looked ahead to see that this Sunday fell on August 6th which is the feast of the Transfiguration. Although we hear about the Transfiguration every year on the second Sunday of Lent, the actual feast of the Transfiguration is on August 6. It is an important enough feast that it replaces the normal Sunday liturgy.

Tradition identifies Mt. Tabor as the mountain of the Transfiguration. It's quite a climb to get to the top.

There is a chapel on top of the mountain commemorating the occasion of the Transfiguration. I said Mass there sixteen years ago when I went with a study group to the Holy Land. They had cars and buses to take us up the mountain. I'm not surprised that Peter, James and John fell asleep, as St. Luke tells us in his gospel, when they went there with Jesus. They didn't have cars and buses and they would have been very tired when they got to the top. But when they woke up their efforts to make it up to the top of that mountain with Jesus were well rewarded. "It is good that we are here," Peter said. "Let us make three tents here: one for you, one for Moses and one for Elijah." It sounds to me as if they were ready to stay there for several weeks, it was such an awesome experience. As wonderful as it was, Jesus' work wasn't finished and neither was theirs. They had to come back down to earth.

Most of us, I'm sure, have had moments when we've felt God's presence and closeness and special love, or when we knew God was helping us with some problem. But I'm sure there are few, if any of us, who have experienced anything like the Transfiguration. We may be a mystic and have ecstatic experiences in prayer or we may be a saint who receives visions of Jesus or Mary. Other than that, we've probably not experienced anything like the Transfiguration and may find it difficult to relate to. But we can learn from it.

(1) We can learn that God has great glory reserved for us until, as the second reading tells us, "day dawns and the morning star rises in your hearts."

(2) We can learn from what God spoke on the holy mountain about Jesus: "this is my beloved Son, listen to him." This is not something new, of course, but it doesn't hurt to be reminded once again that we must listen to him.

(3) We can learn that we cannot expect mountain-

top experiences every day when we pray, when we receive the sacraments, when we keep the Commandments. There are those moments when we get a lot of consolation and good feelings from our faith and our prayers. Then there are those moments when prayer is dry, when our faith is exactly what that word means, believing only on the word of another and not feeling anything except that we're in a desert. The apostles were with Jesus three years and there was only one experience like the Transfiguration, and only three of them experienced it. Our religion can't be based on feelings. It's based on faith in God and love for God and for one another. Sometimes we feel it and sometimes we don't. It's not how we feel it that counts, but how we live it.

(4) Another thing we can learn from the Transfiguration is that we can't always trust appearances. In appearance Jesus looked pretty much like the rest of us. Artists have pictured him with a halo, but I'm sure there was no halo when people saw him every day. The gospels would have remarked about it if there were. For a brief moment on Mt. Tabor, the apostles saw and heard things that indicated there was a lot more to Jesus than they ever imagined.

Today, as we come to Mass, our faith calls us to look beyond appearances. When we receive Communion, we receive what appears to be a wafer of bread and a sip of wine, but faith in the power and the words of Jesus tells us this host and cup offers us so much more. It is food for eternal life. We pray as always that the Lord will help us to know his presence with us today, and if we do not experience that presence, we pray for the faith to be able to see beyond appearances and still be able to say as Peter did on the mountain: "it is good that we are here."

19th Sunday in Ordinary Time

August 9, 2009

INTRODUCTION – (1 Kings 19:4-8; Eph. 4:30; John 6:41-51) Jezebel was an evil queen who reigned in Israel eight hundred fifty years before Christ. One of her many goals in life was to eliminate faith and worship of the God Yahweh in Israel. At the same time there also lived in Israel the prophet Elijah who was dedicated to serving Yahweh. Naturally these two would clash. Elijah had just worked a powerful miracle on Mt. Carmel, a place now known as Haifa, which dramatically demonstrated that Yahweh was truly God, and that the gods Jezebel promoted were non-existent. Jezebel, instead of being converted, became a sore loser she sent her army after Elijah to kill him. Elijah quickly left the place. He ran to the desert in southern Judea and this is where we meet him in today's first reading. He is hungry, tired and deeply depressed. You will hear that God did not desert his faithful prophet. Mt. Horeb, mentioned in the first reading, is the mountain where God gave Moses the Ten Commandments.

This passage has been chosen because it tells us of a special food God gave Elijah. The passage connects with the gospel where Jesus tells us he is the bread that will strengthen us on our journey through life and into eternal life.

HOMILY – The angel told Elijah: "Get up and eat, else the journey will be too long for you." What must have been in those hearth cakes? Talk about energy drinks and power bars! The Jews ate hearth cakes a lot, which I believe were something like tortillas. No one knows the hidden ingredient in those hearth cakes the angel offered Elijah.

Jesus is offering the people of his own day a food infinitely more potent than Elijah's hearth cakes: "bread that comes down from heaven so that one may eat it and not die...whoever eats this bread will live forever." If a person really believed this, wouldn't they make sure they had a steady diet of this marvelous food? But Jesus' hearers thought he had flipped out, making such outlandish claims.

Let's suppose a nutritionist from our own time got into a time machine and went back to talk with those people. And the nutritionist told them that certain foods were especially healthy for them and too much of other foods like saturated fat and salt and sugar would lead to numerous types of disease. Our imaginary nutritionist would explain that there are tiny things in food which they cannot see but which will produce good or bad effects on their health. They won't see those effects right away but the good or bad effects of what they eat will show up a few years later, and maybe not even for several years. And lastly the people are told that if the food tastes really wonderful, it's probably not good for them. The nutritionist would probably be considered ridiculous. People wouldn't be able to understand a message like that. Today we know a lot about food and its consequences, even if we don't always follow what we know we should do. Jesus is telling us there is something in the food he offers that will benefit us eternally. It is we who would be the loser if we ignore what he says.

This is one of the greatest tests of our faith in Jesus – to believe something we can't understand, to believe it simply because we trust the one who told us it is so. It's no wonder our Lord tells us we need God's help to accept this, for as he says: "no one can come to me unless the Father who sent me draw him."

I have lived with this mystery since I made my first Communion at St. Patrick's Church here in Northside in the second grade. Many times I have questioned how this could be. How could bread and wine become the body and blood of Christ. I want to tell you some of the things that have helped my faith. I received a lot of help believing in the Eucharist through meditation on this sixth chapter of John. An article by a psychoanalyst, Ignace Lepp, who was originally an atheist and a Communist and who later became a Catholic priest helped the Eucharist make much more sense to me. I was helped by reading about a German mystic, Teresa Neumann, who died in 1962 who lived for 36 years without any food other than the Eucharist. The Nazi authorities took away her food rations' card during World War II for this reason. From what I've read, I am satisfied that her fasting on nothing but the Eucharist has been verified scientifically. You can look up more information about her on the internet. I have been helped by the deep peace I often feel when I pray before the Blessed Sacrament. I frequently have sensed Jesus' presence. And finally I have been helped by simply choosing to take Jesus at his word: "This is my body" and "this is my blood."

I've never had visions or ecstasies. I have to believe in the Eucharist as much as any of you. Sometimes I think it requires more faith for me, when I realize my own faults and weaknesses and failures and to think that I can say those words of Jesus over bread and wine and at that moment the bread and wine is changed to become Jesus himself.

Elijah didn't know what was in those hearth cakes. In faith, he ate them and began his journey to Mt. Horeb as the angel directed him to do. We have been told what is in the food Jesus offers us, that it is Jesus himself. We just have to do what the angel told Elijah: "get up and eat, else the journey will be too long." We skip meals sometimes when we're in a hurry, but this is one meal we can't skip. We need the strength it gives us as we make our journey to eternal life. Amen.

Feast of the Assumption
August 14/15, 2000

INTRODUCTION AT THE VIGIL: (1 Chr 15:3-4, 15-16; 16:1-2; 1 Cor 15:5b-57; Luke 11:27-28) It is a dogma of our faith that at the end of her life, Mary, like her son, was taken body and soul into heaven. This is the meaning of the Assumption, whose vigil we celebrate this evening.

Our first reading is about the Ark of the Covenant, the sacred gold plated box that contained the Ten Commandments and on top of which were two golden angels (similar to the two angels on our tabernacle doors if you can see them.) The Ark was the unique symbol of God's presence with Israel. It was constructed in the desert after Moses and the Israelites left Egypt. It led them into the Promised Land. Often it was taken into battle with them. When King David established his capital in Jerusalem about the year 1000 BC, he brought the Ark there. Today's reading describes this solemn and joyful occasion. After the temple was built, the Ark was placed in the Holy of Holies and there it remained for 400 years until the Babylonians destroyed the temple.

In Christian symbolism, Mary is sometimes referred to as the Ark of the Covenant. As the Ark represented the special presence of God dwelling with his people, Mary carried within herself Jesus who is truly Son of God dwelling with us.

INTRODUCTION ON THE FEAST: (Rev 11:19a; 12:1-6a, 10ab; 1 Cor 15:20-27; Luke 1: 39-56) It is a dogma of our faith that at the end of her life, Mary, like her son, was taken body and soul into heaven. This is the meaning of the Assumption, the feast we celebrate today.

In our first reading from Revelation, we hear about a woman, a child and a dragon. The dragon is the devil and the powers of evil at work in the world. The child is Christ. The woman in our reading has a double symbolism. She stands for Mary, the physical mother of Jesus Christ and she stands for the Church, our spiritual mother who brings Jesus Christ to birth in us through faith and the sacraments. The glorious way in which the woman is described has a double symbolism too. It symbolizes the glory of Mary in the assumption and it also symbolizes the glory which we, the faithful, the Church, hope to enjoy one day.

HOMILY – St. Francis de Sales asks the simple question in his sermon for the Assumption: "What son would not bring his mother back to life and would not bring her into paradise after her death if he could?" Who could argue with a statement like that? In Mary's Assumption the glory of Jesus' resurrection is first of all extended to his mother, but as we celebrate it we celebrate likewise our own hope to share in this risen glory some day. We recite this belief in the last lines of the creed: "We believe in the resurrection of the dead, and the life of the world to come."

It's interesting that the Holy Father declared the dogma of the Assumption during a difficult time in recent history. In 1950, when the doctrine of the Assumption was declared by Pope Pius XII, we had experienced two world wars, the Holocaust, the Atomic

Bomb and the beginning of the Cold War. The world had enough reason to feel hopeless. Contrasted with the pessimism of the time, this dogma offers hope, hope that the destiny of the human race is more than wars, destruction and devastation. At about that same time in 1950, the cult of the body and the glories of sexuality were beginning to take hold of society. The Church leaders could see that the more that sex and the body were idolized the more society would lose its respect for marriage and family values. In contrast to the glorification of the body as an object of pleasure, this dogma affirms the true dignity and the beauty of the body and the source of that dignity and beauty which is God's grace within us.

In the Assumption Mary is fully united with her son in glory. She remains his mother. He remains her son. Cardinal Suenens once said, "Jesus does not point out Mary and say, 'She used to be my mother.'" Not only is she Jesus' mother, she is our mother too, for on Calvary Jesus gave her to us to be our mother. "Woman, behold your son," he said to her and to St. John, who was a representative of all disciples, Jesus said "Behold your mother." We know and believe that Mary is concerned about our salvation. We expect Mary to help us and we pray to her. Protestants sometimes have trouble with this idea of praying to Mary. Jesus is our savior and we all believe that. But Protestants believe we should pray for one another. If we can ask others to pray for us and we pray for them, why can't those in heaven also pray for us? Are we now so separated from those who have died so that they no longer can help us or be concerned about us? If we seek the prayers of sinners on earth, for we are all sinners, why not seek the intercession of the saints in heaven? Why not turn to the Queen of saints, God's own Mother?

The Assumption tells us that God is not only concerned about our souls but also about our bodies. They are temples of the Spirit. They are part of who we are, and so the feast of the Assumption is a feast that celebrates who we shall be.

In addition to the Arc of the Covenant being a symbol for Mary, there is an another way in which today's first reading connects with today's feast. In Christian literature, especially in the book of Revelation, Jerusalem symbolizes our heavenly home. Thus, the Ark being taken to Jerusalem symbolized Mary being taken body and soul into the heavenly kingdom.

20th Sunday in Ordinary Time

August 16, 2009

INTRODUCTION – (Proverbs 9:1-6; Ephesians 5:15-20; John 6:51-58) The ninth chapter of the book of Proverbs speaks of two women – not real women but both are symbols: one is the symbol of wisdom and one the symbol of foolishness. Thus they are named Lady Wisdom and Dame Folly. Each is pictured as the owner of an inn, and both are busy inviting people to stay at their inn and partake of the meal they have prepared. Those who share the hospitality of Lady Wisdom are rewarded with joy and an abundance of life. Those who accept the invitation of Dame Folly are walking into a trap that will result in death. We hear in today's first reading only the first part of chapter nine in Proverbs: the invitation of Lady Wisdom. The columns that are part of her house symbolize stability, while the number seven symbolizes perfection.

HOMILY – I want to start off with something I've been wanting to tell all of our people for a long time:

Thank you for being here today. It is always a wonderful experience for me to pray with you. I know that three-fourths of you come from outside of Northside, so you are here because you want to be here. I am grateful for your faith, your prayer and your presence. I am grateful every Sunday, even if I don't say it. Today we hear in the gospel one of the most important reasons why we are all here, to be fed by the body and blood of Christ. It is food that promises life eternal.

Before I talk about today's gospel, I want to say a little more about the first reading from Proverbs. The book of Proverbs was written as an instruction for young people, to guide them as they mature. It stresses education, self-discipline, prudence, honesty, good moral character - all of which lead to wisdom. Folly is not just silliness but is a lack of self-control and self-discipline, a conceited attitude, laziness, irreverence, living only for the moment. As I said earlier, wisdom and folly are symbolized in the book of Proverbs as two women calling out to people, especially the young, to partake of the banquet they offer – the first leading to life, the other to the grave. We only heard about Lady Wisdom in today's first reading. Her message is "come, eat of my food and drink of the wine I have mixed! Forsake foolishness that you may live." The words obviously apply to today's gospel where Jesus tells us in a variety of ways that we must eat of the food and drink he offers us (his own body and blood) that we may have eternal life. Coming to him is the way to a wisdom which is beyond this world. Prudence uses the term "fool" to describe a person who can help themselves by choosing the path to wisdom but chooses otherwise. We tend to think of a "fool" as a person who can't help themselves - a person who is mentally limited, who sees things superficially. We call a person "wise" who can see beyond the obvious. We all know that wisdom involves more than innate ability; it is that. It also has to be developed through education, instruction, self-discipline and hard work. When you think of wise people, whom might you think of? I think of people like Socrates, Aristotle, St. Augustine, St. Thomas Aquinas, musicians like Bach, Mozart, Beethoven, Mendelssohn, artists like DaVinci and Michelangelo. One of the first categories of wise people who came to mind when I was thinking of people who see beyond the obvious, the inventor, there are many: Edison, Bell, Geo. Washington Carver, Whitney, Madam Curie, Gutenberg, Einstein, Jonas Salk, Galileo, Morse. I can't overlook our own former parishioner and alumnus of St. Boniface School: Dr. Thomas Fogarty. His name you will find under famous inventors alphabetically listed right above Henry Ford and Ben Franklin. I also cannot overlook some of our own parents and grandparents who might never be famous but who were sources of wisdom for us. These were all people who were not only bright but who worked hard to see what was not obvious to others and who made our life in this world better, safer, easier, healthier, more productive, more fulfilling, more beautiful.

Jesus is telling us there are some things we cannot see on our own, even some things that are not obvious even after he tells us about it. If we allow ourselves to be guided by his word, it will make our life more wonderful and it will be forever. He invites everyone to come to him to be enlightened. Without his light our vision will be limited to what we can figure out on our own. With his light we see further – into eternity. A shortcut to this wisdom he offers us is the Eucharist.

I hardly need to explain today's gospel. It could not be more clear: "Unless you eat the flesh of the Son of Man and drink his blood, you do not have life within you." The Eucharist is not just a one-time event, any more than eating a one time healthy meal will make us healthy. The Eucharist is a way of life by which we allow ourselves to be constantly nourished with Jesus' body and blood. "Whoever eats my flesh and drinks my blood remains in me and I in him." And he "will have life because of me." Amen.

21st Sunday in Ordinary Time

August 23, 2009

INTRODUCTION – (Joshua 24:1-2a, 15-17, 18b; Eph 5:21-32; John 6:60-69) Shortly after God's people arrived in the Promised Land, Joshua, who became their leader after Moses died, gathered the people together to renew their covenant with Yahweh. They enthusiastically chose to commit themselves to follow God faithfully. History tells us later generations did not remain so enthusiastically faithful. In contrast with this commitment of fidelity, we hear in today's gospel that many of Jesus' disciples chose not to follow him after his teaching on the Eucharist.

Husbands, when you hear today's second reading, don't start nudging your wives when you hear Paul say "wives should be subordinate to their husbands." First of all keep in mind the first sentence where Paul says to both husbands and wives: "Be subordinate to one another?? You might notice too that Paul is just as demanding (and maybe even more so) of husbands in this passage than he is of wives. Married love involves commitment and mutuality. In the end, it should resemble the love between Christ and the Church.

HOMILY – For five weeks now our gospel reading has been from the beautiful sixth chapter of St. John. The sixth chapter began with Jesus feeding a great crowd with just five loaves of bread and two fish. It developed further with Jesus telling the crowd that he had a better food he wanted to offer them, the bread of life, which was himself. We heard Jesus insist last week "whoever eats my flesh and drinks my blood has eternal life and I will raise him on the last day." His listeners respond as we heard in today's gospel: "This is a hard saying, who can accept it?" and they started walking away. If anyone doubts as to whether Jesus wanted them to take him literally when he said "this is my body," this passage should take away all doubts. Jesus didn't call his followers who were leaving him to come back. He didn't say "you misunderstood me. What I said I meant symbolically." He knew they heard him clearly and they understood him perfectly. He let them go their way. He just asked the Apostles, "are you going to leave me too?"

Last week or the week before, I can't remember which, someone came up to me after Mass and said "I don't see why you are spending so much time trying to explain that Christ is really present in the Eucharist. I've never doubted it." I thought that's good that this person had such strong and simple faith. But not everyone has such unquestioned faith. A great number of us, as we mature, have all kinds of questions about faith and we are open to any support we can get that our faith is for real. That's what I tried to offer. There is a second purpose why I spent a lot of time talking about the real presence of Christ in the Eucharist. St. Peter tells us that we should always be ready to give an explanation to anyone who asks us for a reason why we have the faith and hope that we have. (1 Peter 3:15)

As I was saying Mass this week, I was inspired to reflect on why Jesus feeds us under two forms: body and blood. Wouldn't one be enough? Theologically it is.

When we receive Christ under either form, we receive the living, risen, glorified body of Christ as he exists now. Jesus said last week, "Just as the living Father sent me and I have life because of the Father, so also the one who feeds on me will have life because of me." Our union with Jesus, who is living, gives eternal life to our spirits, just as the union of a branch to the vine gives life to the branch. The consecrated bread, as it represents food, tells us the Eucharist is nourishing and life-giving, and in the Jewish mind the blood especially tells us that. In the Jewish mind life was in the blood. That's why the Jews were not allowed to drink blood. It had to be poured on the ground because life came from God and it had to return to God. Jewish dietary laws, which the Apostles carefully followed, required all Jews to drain the blood from any meat they ever ate. It must have been a real shock to the Apostles at the Last Supper when Jesus handed them the cup and said to them to drink his blood.

I have drifted away from what I started to say which was why Jesus gave himself to us under two forms: body and blood. It is meant to remind us of his death for us. As he said "This is my body which will be given for you This cup is the new covenant in my blood, which will be shed for you." (Lk. 22:19-20) When a person's blood is no longer in their body they are dead. When we participate in the Eucharist, we are not only reminded that Jesus died for us but we somehow are united with the saving power of Jesus' loving and perfect sacrifice of himself to the Father. As Paul tells us "as often as you eat this bread and drink the cup, you proclaim the death of the Lord until he comes." (1 Cor 11:26) When we participate in Mass, we place our own lives on the altar, along with all the things we suffer and all the things for which we are grateful. In love we offer ourselves to the

Father along with Jesus.

This may be a challenge for many people to grasp. When we believe something we cannot understand or we cannot prove, when we believe it simply because someone we trust told us, we call that faith. This was the faith Peter showed when Jesus asked the Apostles if they were going to leave. He responded: "Master, to whom shall we go?" He didn't understand what Jesus was saying any better than those who were leaving Jesus but, as he said: "We have come to believe and are convinced that you are the Holy One of God." Sometimes Peter put his foot in his mouth, but this time he answered perfectly. It is as good an answer as we could give to anyone as to why we're here today. Amen.

22nd Sunday in Ordinary Time
August 30, 2009

INTRODUCTION – (Deut 4:1-2, 6-8; Jas 1:17-18, 21-22, 27; Mark 7:1-8, 14-15, 21-23) Today's first reading takes us back about 13 centuries before Christ. God's people, after their escape from Egypt and their 40 year sojourn in the desert, are getting close to crossing the Jordan and entering the Promised Land. Moses was still with them and he knew he would die before they crossed the Jordan. So he had some last words instructing and encouraging God's people before his departure. In essence he is telling God's people that God loves his people and he wants them to prosper. They will do so only if they keep God's laws. This passage fits well with the second reading which tells us to be doers of the word and not hearers only and it leads into the gospel where Jesus reminds us that the essence of all law is love.

HOMILY – It's obvious that Mark was writing for Gentiles, in that he had to explain a number of Jewish customs. We all know it is a good idea to wash our hands before we eat, but in Jesus' day, failure to do so made a person a sinful person according to the Pharisees. It was not a written law found in the Bible, but a tradition. Often their traditions contradicted the written law of God and Jesus didn't hesitate to point that out to his adversaries. In today's gospel, Jesus went further than correcting the Pharisees for ignoring God's word. Jesus made an interpretation of God's Law that was among the most shocking things he said to the people of his day. He told them "nothing that enters a person from outside can defile that person;" i.e., it cannot turn them into a sinful person.

Abstinence from certain foods was required by Mosaic Law; it was a stronger mandate than a tradition of the elders such as washing hands before eating. In the concluding line in today's gospel, Jesus states that what a person eats does not make that person unholy, but it's what comes out of one's heart that makes us unholy. In effect he eliminated a long standing Old Testament Law. At the same time he reminded us that God sees in our hearts what we truly are.

Jesus, of course, spoke with divine authority when he declared all foods clean. Jesus, as far as we know, never carried out his own principle of disregarding dietary laws. His followers, however, as we learn from the Acts of the Apostles, under the guidance of the Spirit, applied this principle to their preaching of the gospel, especially when Gentiles started coming into the Church.

All of this may seem meaningless to us today, but it's not. We all know how important it is that we behave in a manner that is appropriate and kind. We must be "doers of the word and not hearers only," as St. James tells us in today's second reading, or we are deluding ourselves that we are pleasing to God. Here Jesus is reminding all of us that, important as our behavior is, there's something even more important: and that is what's in our heart. What should be in our heart? Love! Love for God and for each other – which Jesus tells us are the two greatest commandments. Jesus tells us this is where his hearers went wrong. They were doing all the right things, more or less, but he tells them, quoting Isaiah: "This people honors me with their lips, but their hearts are far from me."

That long list of evils that may come out of our hearts, which Jesus talks about, may make us think we're going to be in big trouble all the time. But we're not in big trouble all the time because we're not perfect all the time. We get distracted in prayers, we get angry at people sometimes and maybe feel like strangling them, we may feel greedy or envious or proud, we might allow temptations against purity to hang around for a while too long. Christ came to us, not because we're perfect, but because we need his help to please God. He will help us if we ask him. What Jesus wants to do is to fill our hearts with his love. Out of this love he desires that we love and serve God and treat one another in a kind and loving way.

Indeed, that's a big order, the job of a lifetime. Perhaps as we continue on with the Mass, we can be aware of our external actions and do them not in a mechanical sort of way, but with adoration and love for the one who loves us infinitely and eternally. Amen.

23rd Sunday in Ordinary Time

September 6, 2009

INTRODUCTION – (Isaiah 35:4-7; Jas 2:1-5; Mark 7:31-37) The prophet Isaiah is speaking to God's people during their captivity in Babylon: "Be strong, fear not! Here is your God, he comes to save you." God's salvation is expressed in terms of healing the blind and the deaf, the lame and the mute. The desert would come alive with rivers and springs and an abundance of life-giving water. The reading prepares us for the gospel where Jesus heals a man who was a deaf mute. Jesus' healing work was a work of compassion, but it also announced in a dramatic way God's saving presence among his people. In our own times of trial, we need to remind ourselves over and over again of these words of Isaiah: "Here is your God, he comes to save you."

HOMILY – Two years ago in January the Washington Post conducted an experiment you may have heard about. The experiment involved Joshua Bell, one of the world's greatest violinists who performed for almost all the world's orchestras. Joshua Bell was commissioned to play his $4,000,000 Stradivarius violin in a subway station in Washington, DC. So he dressed like a street musician looking for tips and sat in the subway station playing for 45 minutes. The Washington Post had a hidden camera to video the entire event. Out of the 1097 people who passed by him, seven stopped to listen! He received $32.17 in tips not counting the $20 he received from one person who recognized him.

The story would be an excellent illustration of what St. James tells us in today's second reading, but I prefer to use this story to illustrate today's gospel. I am presuming that those 1097 people who passed by Joshua Bell had good hearing, but their ability to know what to listen for wasn't very well developed - at least not in the area of music.

Jesus healed a man in today's gospel who was deaf. What a gift Jesus gave him! He could suddenly hear which is amazing. But he still had a lot of catching up to do to learn how to listen, how to recognize, for example, sounds that warn of immanent danger, how to recognize not only words but also nuances in the tone of a person's voice, how to recognize sounds from nature, how to learn what unfamiliar words mean.

We who are blessed with hearing are sometimes not good listeners. This happens in families a lot: spouses with each other, children with parents and vice versa. This happens with God too. He hears us, ("shall he who made the ear not hear?") but we do not always hear him. That's why we need to keep reading the Scriptures over and over, because when we do we discover there is more and more that they can teach us. That's why we need to take quiet time to pray, because there's so much noise around us and God usually speaks in a very quiet voice. As a matter of fact, I've always found that God speaks in thoughts rather than words. When our thoughts are always being pushed and pulled by all the noise around us (including visual noise) thoughts from God do not seem to get through.

The guidance I received that helped me in my relationship with God came from good spiritual books, inspiring speakers and teachers, wise friends, a good confessor, renewal programs and retreats for which I must give credit. Notice in today's gospel, the deaf man's friends brought him to Jesus and begged Jesus to lay his hands on him. We need good books and friends and people in our lives who can lead us to Jesus by their faith and sometimes we have to be the person who leads others to Jesus, but at the same time there is no substitute for quiet time. Notice when Jesus healed the man he took him aside – away from the crowd. We need to get away from the crowd each day to spend a little while in silence with our Lord. Quiet time has been essential to me ever since I can remember, helping to keep me going through difficult times, giving me ideas when I had an issue I couldn't figure out, helping me with what I needed to say to a person needing help, allowing me to experience God's loving presence.

Jesus worked many miracles of healing and he still does. In the gospels we read he healed people because of his compassion, in response to a request, in response to faith, to demonstrate that God's kingdom was present. He healed people to show in a visible way the blessings he wanted to give to us that were not visible. Jesus helped this man to hear, and in doing so he shows us what his primary mission was, to teach us how to hear and how to listen to God. Let us ask God to open the ears of our hearts to his word and to his love as we continue offering Mass today. Amen.

24th Sunday in Ordinary Time

September 13, 2009

INTRODUCTION – (Isaiah 50:5-9; James 2:14-18; Mark 8:27-35) The book of the prophet Isaiah contains four poems commonly referred to as Servant Songs. They are mysterious passages because no one is sure whom they referred to originally. They describe one whom God had chosen from before birth - not only to serve God and to serve God's people in Israel, but to be a light to all nations. It's amazing how perfectly these Servant Songs, written over 500 years before Christ, describe Jesus. Today's passage describes how God's Servant would encounter resistance, persecution and martyrdom, and how God would stand by him during all his trials. We hear this same passage again on Palm Sunday and on Wednesday of Holy Week. It was chosen for today because we hear Jesus predict in today's gospel that suffering, death and resurrection are ahead for him.

HOMILY – Caesarea Philippi is one of the places I visited in the Holy Land 20 years ago. I still remember it well. It is in northern Galilee near where the Jordan river begins. The area in not dry like most of Israel, but it is lush with much vegetation and water. There is a shrine there that was dedicated to the Greek god, Pan. The shrine is carved into a high cliff, along with a number of other niches, which held statues of Greek and Roman gods and goddesses. It was in this setting that Jesus asked his disciples, "Who do people say I am?" Then he asked, "Who do you say I am?" Here is the Son of God asking, "We see ourselves surrounded by all these gods and goddesses. Who do you say that I am?" Peter said, "You are the Christ, i.e., you are the Messiah, the long awaited savior." The word Messiah is from the Hebrew, which designated one who was anointed, that is: a king or a priest. The Greek word for Messiah is Christos. Jesus told them not to tell anyone about him; Jesus may have had several reasons why he didn't want them to tell others about him, but one reason is obvious from the gospels: Peter could recognize Jesus as Messiah, but he really had only a limited idea of what Messiah meant. Jesus instructed them that it meant Jesus would have to suffer if he were going to save the people – an idea Peter rejected and for which Jesus severely reprimanded him.

It is this problem of suffering that is precisely where a lot of people lose faith in God or lose faith in Christ. We see so much suffering around us and we ask, "Why doesn't God put a stop to all this suffering?" or "Why does Christ allow this or that tragedy to happen?" I was asking myself this question Friday while thinking of what happened on 9/11/2001. Like Peter we want to say: "This cannot be."

Most of us have a favorite way of picturing Jesus: as

Savior, or an understanding friend, or a merciful and forgiving person, a great teacher, a powerful healer, a good shepherd, as the Sacred Heart, an advocate for the poor, an eternal king, the Son of God, a great storyteller. But to think of him in his sufferings and as one who tells us if we want to follow him we might have to suffer too – that's not an image many people like to dwell on. I know from my own experience that when I am suffering, it is very comforting to think of how Jesus suffered. Other than Lent, I don't believe most people reflect much on Christ as our suffering savior. The gospels, especially today's gospel, tells us that's a big part of who Jesus is and that's how he saved us all.

It's so much a part of who he is it's the principal way he asked us to remember him. He gave us his body to eat - his body which he gave for us, and his blood to drink - his blood which he shed for us; and he said "do this in remembrance of me." I wonder if this is perhaps the reason why people so easily excuse themselves from Mass, because, like Peter, they still have to learn about the mystery and the power of the cross. Like Peter most of us want a Messiah (a Christ) who will take away our problems - not one who has to suffer and who tells us to take up our cross if we wish to follow him.

Let me conclude with two points. First of all, I want to say something about suffering. Simply because we are human, we're going to face suffering of one kind or another. Do not think following Christ will make your crosses in life any heavier, on the contrary it will make them lighter and easier to bear. Peter hadn't come to that understanding yet in today's gospel, but eventually he did.

The final point is that when Jesus said "whoever wishes to save his life will lose it and whoever loses his life for my sake will save it," does not mean we all have to be martyrs if we want to get to heaven. What Jesus said about losing one's life was literally true in many cases in the early Church when there were persecutions, and it is literally true in some parts of the world today. We must be willing to hold on to our faith even in the face of death. But for people in 21st century in countries where there is religious freedom, we need to understand that losing our life for Christ means basically losing the selfish, proud, negative, unholy side of ourselves so that we can be the kind of person who pleases God. In this we will be saved.

In the question "who do you say that I am?" it's not enough just to be able to give the right answer. The gospels show us that coming to know Jesus is an on-going process throughout our lives. It's a matter of getting to know him better and not trying to make him into who we want him to be. Amen.

Feast of the Holy Cross

September 14, 2008

INTRODUCTION – (Numbers 21:4b-9; Philippians 2:6-11; John 3: 13-17) Our first reading takes us back over a thousand years before Christ, to the time when Moses was leading God's people from slavery in Egypt to the freedom of the Promised Land. The trip through the desert was extremely difficult and at times the people complained bitterly. One of their difficulties was an encounter with a nest of poisonous serpents whose bite brought intense suffering and burning pain and then death. The serpents were called saraph serpents, for saraph means "fiery." The people saw this as punishment for their complaining. But God gave them a way to be healed from the serpent's bite. The remedy might remind us of the symbol often used today as an icon of the medical profession. In today's gospel, Jesus compares this event to his crucifixion.

HOMILY – During Holy Week we focus on the sufferings of Christ crucified. Today our focus is more on the glory and victory of the cross. In Jesus' day the cross was an instrument of torture, brutality and shame. The Romans reserved it for the worst criminals and enemies of the Roman Empire. If a criminal was a Roman citizen, he or she was exempt from crucifixion because it was such a terrible way to die. Roman citizens were simply beheaded. But Jesus has turned the cross into a symbol of victory, a symbol of hope, a symbol of sacrifice and infinite love. St. Paul tells us in Galatians (2:20) "I live by faith in the Son of God who has loved me and given himself up for me."

Over and over the Scriptures tell us through the cross Jesus saved us, but early Christian art seldom pictured the cross. They didn't need to. Father Foley in *Saint of the Day* said: "It stood outside too many city walls, decorated only with decaying corpses, as a threat to anyone who defied Rome's authority." Included in this group of those who defied Rome's authority were the Christians who would not worship pagan gods, but only the Father, the Lord Jesus and the Spirit. The emperor Constantine who made Christianity legal in 313 also eliminated crucifixion as a form of capital punishment. Once the Roman Empire actually ceased crucifying people, then images of the cross appeared in Christian art. These first images of the cross did not include an image of the suffering Christ, but they were crosses decorated with jewels and precious metals. Incidentally it was a vision of the cross that led to the conversion of Constantine. He was assured in the vision that in the sign of the cross he would conquer Maxentius, a rival to the throne, and he would become emperor of Rome.

Once Constantine gained control of the Roman

Empire, he went to the Holy Land with his mother, St. Helen, to discover the places where Jesus lived and died. Constantine and his mother had churches built in Bethlehem and the Mount of Olives but the most famous church he built is the Church of the Holy Sepulcher, built over the hill of Calvary and the tomb of Jesus. It was in the process of building the Church of the Holy Sepulcher that Jesus' cross was found. How did they know it was Jesus' cross? Legend has it that the men working on this project found three crosses and they didn't know which one was Jesus' cross. They touched each of the crosses to a woman who was dying and when she was touched with the third cross, she was instantly healed. Today's feast of the Holy Cross goes back to that time, around the year 320 AD. It celebrates the finding of the true cross and the dedication of the Basilica of the Holy Sepulcher. So that's why this feast is celebrated in the middle of September and not during Lent as we might expect.

Today's gospel is sometimes called the gospel in miniature. These few verses express the essence of the entire gospel: God's offer of eternal life through the sacrifice of Christ, a sacrifice offered out of love for us. God so loved the world, God so loved you and me that he gave us the greatest gift, the gift of his son, so we would know the greatest blessing: eternal happiness with him.

Today we approach the cross not with sorrow but with joy, not as a symbol of death but of life, not as a sign of defeat but of victory, not as a cause for fear but of hope, not as an instrument of cruelty and hatred but of eternal love. On a practical level, I know somehow it was inevitable if Jesus were to be true to his mission. If he had run away from it, he would not have risen and his message would have soon been forgotten. Today Christians make up one third of the world's population.

If Jesus had abandoned his mission to change the world through love, perhaps some obscure history book might have had a sentence or two about this person who did a lot of healing and was a good preacher, but for the most part his ministry would be forgotten. This is just a superficial explanation of the mystery of the cross. There is much more to this mystery, but each of us has to discover it for ourselves. To come to a deeper understanding takes lots of prayer – and that's what the Mass does for us each week, it reminds us of God's love and the hope and joy and freedom and peace and salvation it gives us. Amen.

25th Sunday in Ordinary Time

September 20, 2009

INTRODUCTION – (Wisdom 2:12, 17-20; James 3:16-4:3; Mark 9:30-37) In 333 BC, Alexander the Great conquered everything between Egypt and India. For a little over 250 years, the Greeks controlled all of the Middle East including the Holy Land. The Greek rulers decided all nations under their rule should accept Greek culture and religion. The Jews were being forced to give up their belief in Yahweh, the one God they had served (not always faithfully) for 1500 years. Those who did not submit were persecuted or killed. Some of the Jews converted to Greek ways and pagan worship and some stayed faithful to Yahweh. The Jews who turned to paganism speak in today's first reading from the Book of Wisdom. They plot against the faithful Jew, sarcastically refer to him or her as "the just one" and ridicule traditional faith in God. The first reading connects with the gospel in that Jesus who is truly the "just one" predicts the suffering he will have to face for remaining faithful to God's work.

HOMILY – The first thing that strikes me about today's gospel is the stark contrast between Jesus and his disciples. Jesus was trying to prepare them for the sufferings he would endure (this was the second time he raised the topic) and they were preoccupied with which of them was the greatest. They just did not understand what Jesus was trying to tell them, and St. Mark tells us, "they were afraid to question him."

Jesus had a lot of big egos in his group. With that attitude they wouldn't make very good disciples, so he had to have a little talk with them. It is easy to imagine that as Jesus is talking with them, there a few children were close by. Jesus motioned to one child to come to him and, putting his arms around the child, Jesus demonstrated the kind of attitude he expected of his followers. In that society children were greatly loved, but they had no social status. They depended totally on the goodwill of their elders. If his disciples were to learn from Jesus and imitate him, they would not be worried about who would be most important in the kingdom; they would become more like Jesus in their thinking. Jesus' attitude was that of service. "If anyone wishes to be first, he shall be the last of all and the servant of all." Jesus himself came "not to be served but to serve" as he would tell them later. (Mk 10:45)

Jesus is not asking us to adopt the attitude that we are not worth anything or that we have no importance. When Jesus said we should love our neighbor as ourselves, he implies that we should love ourselves – otherwise we won't be very good at loving anyone else. As a matter of fact, each of us is of infinite worth because Jesus shed his blood for us, so much does he love us. If all we do is put ourselves down, this will not make us holy, it will just make us depressed. The Christian spirit is a spirit of joy, not depression. We could say that what

Jesus was trying to impress on his disciples was not that they think less of themselves, rather that they think of themselves less. This is an attitude that will help us be more sensitive to the needs of others.

In writing this, I was thinking of Jesus and his service to us. His service to us begins, of course, with creation - with loving us and willing us into being. As we say in the creed: "through him all things were made." Then he, the infinite Son of God, took on our human nature in the womb of Mary. As Paul said, he emptied himself and took on the form of a slave. He spent his public ministry teaching, healing, casting out demons and accepting rejection and abuse for his work of service. He met with hostility from the powers that be and even a gruesome death rather than abandon his work of service. His work of service continues to this day by his presence with us, especially his presence in the Eucharist as he gives us his body and his blood to be our food and source of eternal life.

You've probably all heard this story before about the man who died and went to heaven. He was amazed when he got there to find people he never expected to find. He commented to God: "I never expected to find some of these people here and, by the way, why is everyone so quiet?" God said, "they didn't expect to see you here." Most of us will probably be greatly surprised when we get to heaven and see who is there and who enjoys a more exalted position. We may see the local schoolteacher or fireman or cleaning lady or secretary enjoying a higher rank and greater happiness than kings or generals or millionaires or famous entertainers.

We praise and thank God for all he has done for us. Let us pray we might learn from his example of generous kindness and service to us. Amen.

26th Sunday in Ordinary Time
September 27, 2009

HOMILY – (Nm 11:25-29; Jas 5:1-6; Mark 9:38-43, 45, 47-48) Calvin Coolidge was a man of few words. When he returned from church one Sunday morning his wife asked him what the preacher talked about. Wilson answered "sin." When she asked him what he said about it, he answered "he was agin' it." Dr. Karl Menninger, the world famous psychiatrist who died just a few years ago at the age of 97, wrote a book entitled *Whatever became of sin?* His book begins with a story about a man on a busy street corner in downtown Chicago about 20 years ago. The man was tall, thin, and looked grim and solemn as he watched people walk by. Occasionally he would point a finger at a person coming toward him and say the one word: "guilty." Probably many people who had the finger pointed at them wondered "How does he know?"

That was 20 years ago. If someone were to do something like today I wonder how many would walk away not asking themselves "How does he know?" but asking themselves "I wonder what he means by that?" The thesis of Dr. Menninger's book is that society has lost its sense of sin. In his book *Whatever became of sin?*, Dr. Menninger is not trying to tell us that sin has gone out of existence, but to the contrary, he is telling us it has become a greater problem in society simply because many today are indifferent to the reality of sin.

Yet that is what our readings are about today. Sin is what St. James is speaking of when he talks about social injustice and lack of concern for those in need. Sin is what our Lord is talking about too, when he tells us to cut off our hand, our foot, or tear out our eye if it is going to lead us from God and into damnation. This is a metaphor of course. Our Lord doesn't really intend us to go and mutilate ourselves in this way because sin does not find its origin in our hands or feet but in our mind and heart. Sin is a decision to do something God has forbidden or not to do something God has commanded. In telling us this Jesus is sharing a vision with us that he can see more clearly than any of us can. His vision is that if we want lasting happiness we must hold our relationship with God as more precious than anything else we possess. Especially he emphasizes this with regard to leading little children away from God, not teaching them right, giving them bad example or even abusing them. Think for a moment, this is the gentle, merciful, loving Jesus who is speaking to us when he tells us it would be better for someone to have a great stone tied around their neck and be dropped into the sea rather than lead astray one of God's little ones. Some people want to think Jesus is soft on sin. Truly Jesus is forgiving, but Jesus does not consider sin to be trivial.

Adam and Eve's story in the beginning of the bible is a perfect illustrations of the destructive nature of sin. Adam and Eve were created in a state of happiness, living in peace and harmony with God, with each other and with nature. But they listened to the tempter who told them God gave them rules in order to keep them from greater fulfillment and happiness. To make a long story short, they chose not to trust God and to pursue the happiness they thought God was hiding from them. This failure to trust led to disobedience, and this sin brought to an end the peace and harmony they enjoyed. They could not face God, nor could they face each other. Their innocence was gone. They were embarrassed by their nakedness. Adam tried to blame Eve for his sin while she blamed the serpent. They were even out of harmony with nature. God told them it would only be by sweat and hard work that they would obtain the food they needed. The story tells us sin, any sin, but especially serious sin, harms our relationships with God, with one another and with all of creation.

In scripture, the term for sin that is most often used is a word that means "missing the mark." It is as if someone is shooting an arrow or throwing a ball and their aim is off. Our aim in life, our purpose and our greatest happiness in life will be when all our relationships are perfect, when we are totally one with God, one within our own person (that is, being integrated, not at war within ourselves) and one with each other. This perfect state will be heaven. When we sin, we are missing our real goal in life. We are taking a path that will lead us nowhere near our goal. Theologians have categorized seven different paths we human beings have a tendency to travel that lead us away from our goal. If you remember your catechism, you will recognize them as the seven capital sins: pride, covetousness, lust, anger, gluttony, envy and laziness, especially laziness in our spiritual lives.

Jesus is telling us sin is nothing to play with. It can get a hold on us and not let go easily. There is a story told about a lamb that wandered out onto a frozen section of the Niagara River. The ice broke loose where the lamb was standing, leaving the lamb stranded. Eventually the poor little animal froze to death. An eagle saw the animal and started to make a delicious feast of this fresh frozen lamb. The eagle didn't have to worry that the piece of ice was floating toward the falls. After all, the eagle had powerful wings and could easily fly away. But when the ice floe came to the falls, the eagle discovered that its claws had become frozen in the ice and the eagle went cascading down the falls with the lamb. When we flirt with sin, we tell ourselves we can quit anytime, but often we can't.

When I mentioned to one of our parishioners that I was going to talk about sin, she said "Oh.... I wonder what time St. Ignatius is having Mass this weekend." People devour tabloids and talk shows that reveal the deviant or immoral behavior of others, especially celebrities, but for these same people to come to church and have to listen to a *sermon* on sin is another story. Such a sermon is almost as popular as a sermon on money. If we have sinned, which we all have, this sermon is not intended to make everyone feel guilty. We must remember when God forgives us he also totally forgets. The purpose of this sermon is to call to repentance those who need to repent as well as to remind all of us that sin is a reality and ignoring it will give it a greater hold on us. If we ignore the reality of sin we will also be ignoring the words of Jesus, the gentle Jesus, who tells us in a most emphatic way that it is something we have to take seriously, because it can destroy for us the eternal happiness he wants for us.

27th Sunday in Ordinary Time

October 5, 2003

HOMILY – (Gn 2:18-24; Heb 2:9-11; Mark 10:2-16) A pastor was called to a local nursing home to perform a wedding. He was met by the anxious groom, and on meeting him the pastor started up a conversation. He asked the old man: "Do you love her?" The old man replied: "Nope." "Is she a good Christian woman?" "I don't know for sure," was the old man's answer. "Well, does she have lots of money?" asked the pastor. "I doubt it." "Then why are you marrying her?" the preacher asked. "'Cause she can drive at night," the old man said.

One of my favorite statements about marriage is this:

The shortest sentence in the English language is "I am," the longest is "I do." I asked a few of my friends if they had some statements they could make about marriage that would help me with my sermon. One man said, "I better not say anything. I'm a married man." One wife said, "It depends on the day whether I'm for it or against it." One widow said, "Enjoy it while you can." Giving up marriage was the major issue I had to deal with before being ordained; and it is the major reason most people do not go into religious life or enter the priesthood.

You know, one of the things the people of Jesus' day admired most about Jesus was that he spoke with authority. He didn't have to quote other rabbis or give other people's opinions when giving the answer to a question. And his authority went beyond what he taught. He spoke with authority too when he healed diseases and cast out demons. One of the things modern people like least about him is that he spoke with authority. They would rather look upon Christ's teachings as opinions or suggestions. Especially this is true with regard to marriage. The attitude of Catholics toward marriage, divorce, sex outside of marriage, cohabitation, homosexuality, etc. is not for the most part formed by what Jesus tells us. It's pretty much formed by the attitude of society. Instead of us being a light for the world as we should be, too many of us take our light and direction from society and overlook the teachings of Christ.

One of the most difficult parts of my job is trying to convince people I have to uphold the rules the Church has about marriage. For one reason or another people often complain: "Why does the Church have all these rules? It looks like the Church is trying to make it hard for people to stay in the Church?" I have to say "I'm sorry; the Church is not trying to make it hard for people. The Church is just trying to be faithful to the teachings of Jesus about marriage." If it's meant to be permanent, why shouldn't the couple put some time into trying to prepare for it properly? If a person was married before and they don't want to bother with an annulment, they expect the Church to just throw Jesus' teaching on marriage out the window because it's too much trouble for them to follow. The Church would not be doing its job if it didn't treat marriage seriously.

When the Jews asked Jesus if it were lawful for a man to divorce his wife, they already believed they knew the answer. Divorce was permitted by Jewish law. But Jesus surprised them. He referred to the original intention God had in creating men and women. They were to provide companionship and love for one another and keep the human race going. And this drive God put in us to procreate is to be exercised in the exclusive, permanent relationship of marriage. As the Scriptures tell us, they become two in one flesh. It is based on this unique kind of union that the Church teaches and has always taught that the only appropriate expression of physical love is in marriage. Sexuality is sacred. It has to have boundaries or it will become little more than pure animal behavior. And without adequate boundaries human society will suffer and we would not be faithful to the teachings of the Scriptures.

One of the things that confuses people is the difference between annulments and divorces. A divorce is a legal matter. It is the declaration by the state that the marriage is ended. Sometimes it is necessary. Sometimes a spouse has to protect himself or herself from serious harm. But I've seen too many that were not necessary, simply because one or the other gave up too soon, or thought someone else looked more interesting. If a couple are not relating well, they can learn. I think too many people expect heaven on earth from their marriage and when it doesn't happen they look elsewhere. The Church does not grant divorces to end a marriage. The Church may grant an annulment after a marriage has broken up. An annulment is a statement that after serious investigation by Church authorities a couple are not obligated to each other under God because there was something seriously lacking in their commitment from the beginning. So often it was that one or the other person was unable or not ready at the time to make the kind of serious commitment marriage requires. It can be a very complicated process and it's best not to make rash judgments about people who could or could not get an annulment.

Part of the problem with marriage today is that it is seen by many people as a private arrangement. Its origin is from God as we heard in the first reading. In marriage two people promise God as well as each other to take each other as husband and wife "for better, for worse, for richer, for poorer, in sickness and in health until death."

I could go on talking a long time about marriage. I've worked with people before marriage. I've counseled couples who were having problems. Marital happiness was the basis for my thesis when I got my degree in psychology. In my own personal struggle with not being able to be married because of the priesthood, I've mellowed a lot. I guess that's old age. I learned that every way of life has its joys and its difficulties. Whether we're married or not, our major task in life is learning how to grow in love. That's what its all about and that will be our joy in this life and in heaven.

28th Sunday Ordinary Time
October 11, 2009

HOMILY – (Wisdom 7:7-11; Heb 4:12-13; Mark 10:17-30) Our gospel today was about the rich young man, and although this would be a good opportunity to give a money talk, I'm not prepared to give one this week, so you can put your wallets away (for now). I really want to explain to you this picture of St. Boniface, which was a recent gift to us. But before I talk about St. Boniface I have an amusing story to tell you. St. Bernard's Church in Winton Place caught on fire recently (that's not the amusing part). It was due to out dated electric and Fr. Shappelle told me there was about $50,000 damage. What is amusing is that Fr. Shappelle credits me with saving the church from burning down entirely. Here's how it happened. He had a funeral coming up around 6:00 pm and went over to church about 2:00 to get things ready. While there in church, he decided to sit down and read my homily book – and he fell asleep. He woke up a short time later coughing on the smoke coming from the fire that had started while he was sleeping. If it weren't for my book putting him to sleep, he would have gone back to the rectory and the fire would have been much worse. I'm glad to know my homilies are so helpful.

Now the picture of St. Boniface. I am often asked why we don't have a picture of St. Boniface here. I always point out our stained glass window of him, and I tell people there is a statue of St. Boniface above the front doors of the church. Recently I spoke with Len Buckley, an artist in Maryland, about a picture and he volunteered to paint one. (I introduced Len and his wife Janet at Mass last Saturday). Janet is a graduate of St. Boniface and a cousin of Fran Klosterman. That is his connection with

St. Boniface. His name is not famous but you come in contact with his art work many times during the week. Every time you handle a piece of US currency that has an oval around the president's picture on the front of the bill, the art work on the front and back of the bill is the work of Len Buckley. (The newer bills do not have the president's picture in an oval – in case you hadn't noticed). Len also competed with 100 other artists to design the back of the Colorado quarter and his design won the competition. So much about the artist.

Now the picture. St. Boniface has a red cloak, not only because he was a bishop, but also because he was a martyr. His miter also indicates he was a bishop. Like the man in today's gospel Boniface, gave up everything to follow Christ. He was not any more German than St. Patrick was Irish. St. Boniface was an English Benedictine monk who could have had a very comfortable life as the abbot of a monastery in England, but he felt called to travel to Germany to work for the conversion of Germanic tribes and to reform the German Church. He had his work cut out for him. When he arrived in Germany in 719 (at the age of 47), paganism was a way of life. Whatever Christianity he found had lapsed into paganism or was mixed with error. The clergy he found were uneducated and lax and ignored the pope and their bishops. Boniface was very successful in his work. Four years after arriving in Germany, he challenged the pagan priests by cutting down an oak tree that was considered sacred to the pagan god, Thor. That is the subject of our stained glass window. The people standing around holding their hands above their heads would have been pagans waiting for Thor to strike him dead, but nothing happened. This led to a lot of conversions. St. Boniface built a chapel from the wood of the tree. In our painting, at the lower right hand corner is the stump of a tree representing the tree he cut down. Next to it is the beginning of an evergreen tree representing the new growth of the Church in Germany. Behind his head we see the dark clouds of paganism begin to blow away as Boniface raises his right hand to bless us and his left hand points to the Scriptures, the Word of God. A dagger is set in the stump to represent the instrument of St. Boniface's martyrdom. In 754, at approximately 82 years of age, St. Boniface and 53 companions were massacred as they traveled into Friesland in northern Holland to confer Confirmation. One version of his martyrdom was that the pagans who killed him thought the boxes he carried with him contained gold, but they found only the archbishop's books and relics. I haven't decided yet where I am going to hang this picture, but I have it here today so I can talk about it. The artist dedicated his painting to Fr. Robert Brungs, a Jesuit who said his first solemn Mass here at St. Boniface in June, 1964.

I can't finish my talk about St. Boniface without a special mention of two other saints: St. Damien of Molokai who cared for the lepers in Hawaii until he died of leprosy at age 49 and St. Jeanne Jugan who started the Little Sisters of the Poor. The Sisters do a wonderful job – I know because my stepmother was there until she died. Ted and Roselyn are in the care of the Little Sisters at their home on Riddle Road. I mention Damien and Jeanne Jugan because they have been canonized today by Pope Benedict. I thought you should know this.

A lot of us here would probably never have heard of Christ, had it not been for courageous and dedicated missionaries like St. Boniface or St. Patrick. We could celebrate the faith that came to us through St. Boniface by going out to a beer garden on his feast, June 5, like the Irish do on March 17. Or we can show our gratitude and support for our faith by helping support missionaries in the world today. We will have the opportunity to do that through our Mission Sunday Collection next week. Another way we give thanks to God for our faith (and for all God's blessings) is through our weekly celebration of the Eucharist, as we do now, for as we all know the word "Eucharist" means "Thanksgiving".

29th Sunday in Ordinary Time

October 18, 2009

INTRODUCTION – (Isaiah 53:10-11; Heb 4:14-16; Mk 10:35-45) There are four unique passages in the Book of Isaiah the Prophet that are referred to as the Servant Songs. They were written over 500 years before Christ, and they tell us about some mysterious person or persons, referred to in the verses simply as God's "servant," whose faithfulness and suffering would bring redemption to many people. Each of these passages describe with amazing accuracy the redemptive work of Jesus who would not be born for another 500 years. We read all four Servant Songs during Holy Week. Just a month ago we heard part of one of the servant songs. Today part of the fourth one is read because it corresponds with Jesus' statement in today's gospel that he came to serve and to give his life as a ransom for many.

HOMILY – If you look in St. Mark's gospel, right before today's passage, Jesus had warned his apostles for the third time about his suffering, death and resurrection that was soon to take place. Now, for the third time, we are told by Mark how the apostles hadn't the slightest idea of what he was talking about. The first time Jesus warned them, Peter told Jesus that what Jesus was talking about (suffering and death) just couldn't happen. After the second time the apostles were arguing over which of them was the most important. Now, after Jesus' third prediction, James and John, two who were among his first followers, the only two who along with Peter had witnessed the raising of the daughter of Jairus back to life, the only two who along with Peter had witnessed the Transfiguration, these two now want to be placed ahead of all the others when Jesus comes into his kingdom. We can't fault them. Aren't we often just as oblivious as they were of what God is doing in our lives? Aren't we at times just as bold as they, coming to God and telling him: "we want you to do for us whatever we ask of you." Jesus, in a kindly way, answers them: "What is it you want me to do for you." And patiently he explains what their request would involve (drinking the cup of suffering he would have to drink) and that it was up to their Heavenly Father to give them what they wanted.

He also took the occasion to teach all of them once more a lesson on how to really become great and important, not by being self-serving, but by serving others just as Jesus came to do.

Being a servant does not mean allowing people to walk all over us. Jesus was not afraid to stand up for himself. A policeman who didn't stop bad guys wouldn't be serving anyone. A parent who always let their child have his own way would be a poor parent and would be doing a disservice to their child. A teacher who would let a student get by with cheating or not doing their work would be a poor servant as well as a poor teacher. In other words, being a servant to others does not always gain us popularity. Jesus knew he was making a lot of enemies by the work he was doing, healing, teaching and attacking the evil spirits. He was, nonetheless, ready to lay down his life in order to serve others, even when people ignored him, misunderstood him, didn't appreciate what he was doing or hated him for it

Why would he do all of that? There was no other reason except love. I'm using the word "love" not to refer to an emotional or sentimental feeling necessarily but as a desire to do what one can do to help others. It's the same kind of love Jesus asks of us: "A new commandment I give you, that you love one another as I have loved you." At the Last Supper Jesus did something to demonstrate to his apostles a lesson he had spent his entire life trying to teach them. He washed the feet of each one of them. Peter, as I'm sure we all remember, objected to having his feet washed by Jesus. Peter felt it was so inappropriate for his master to kneel before him and do this dirty job that was generally done only by slaves. After Jesus had finished he told them: "I have given you an example to follow, so that as I have done for you, you should also do."

This world is made up of givers and takers. You see this in business, in social and family relations. I see it a lot in the Church. As Christians we are called to be givers. Some years ago I attended to a man who was dying of cancer. He dealt with his suffering with a great deal of peace. He told me one of the things that gave him peace was that in life he always tried to give more than he had taken.

We ask the Lord to help us follow his example of love as we celebrate now the love of One who gave his life as a ransom for all of us.

30th Sunday in Ordinary Time

October 25, 2009

HOMILY – (Jeremiah 31:7-9; Heb 5:1-6; Mark 10:46-52) Today we hear about a blind beggar who could actually see who Jesus is more clearly than the disciples and crowd who had been with him all along. It has been my objective every week to lead all of us to a fuller vision of who Jesus is and what he taught. I say "all of us" because I assure you I benefit as much or more than anyone else being able to reflect on the Scripture readings and trying to make them more understandable.

I have always believed that if I try to bring my parishioners to a deeper union with Christ, I will not have to worry about having enough money to run the parish. Ever since I became a pastor 32 years ago in Loveland, that has always been the case. But I would have only myself to blame if I start to worry and lose sleep over our finances without informing our parishioners that we need more support than we are currently receiving. Besides, this is part of my job to let you know how we are doing financially. This topic is just as basic as trying to bring people to a closer union with Christ, because if we're not able to stand on our own financially, the Archbishop will have to say it's time to close the doors for good. The Archdiocese simply does not have the funds to keep parishes open who are unable to keep themselves open. Our situation is not that desperate yet, but I need to tell people where we are before it gets desperate. Everyone I know has felt the effects of the downturn in the economy. Some of our parishioners have lost their jobs, some have been cut back, and some have not received a raise or if they did, it wasn't much of one. Every year for the past several years, around Christmas time, I have reminded people to continue to be generous and our people have been. Evidence of the generosity and commitment of our parishioners is that for the past five years I have not had to give a talk on money. As a matter of fact, in the last 18 years I have been here, there's only been one year, other than this year, that we've come out in the red. I think that was maybe ten or fifteen years ago and we came out about $5000 in the red. This past fiscal year if we had come out $5000 in the red, I would have had a party. Actually this past fiscal year we were down $59,000. Now I'm not going to ask you to try to make up the $59,000 we lost. We'll just hope maybe we'll get some generous bequests in years to come to help build our savings back up to where they were. I bring this topic before you because I don't want it to happen again this year. It could happen, however, if things don't move in a different direction.

Since July 1, the start of this fiscal year, we are down about $6000. We looked to find where we could reduce expenses, and we did reduce our staff by a half-time person. Another thing we did was decide we would probably not be able to help the school to the extent as we have in the past. I would like to say something about the school for a moment. The school is our ministry to the poor. 90% of our school families live below the poverty line and I am proud to say we are giving them a good education to help them succeed better in this world and, hopefully, to help them spiritually to find happiness in the next. We receive considerable help to run the school from State of Ohio vouchers and from our Catholic Inner City School Endeavor (CISE). Both of these sources of income have cut back the amount of help they give us. So the school will have to dip into its reserve just as the parish has had to do. Fortunately, we have some reserves because a parishioner left a nice bequest to the school a couple of years ago, but it will be gone in a couple of years if things don't get better.

Returning to the topic of parish finances: the simple fact is that our expenses have gone up and our collections have gone down. Bequests and special gifts have also gone down considerably. I'm not going to bore you with all the details of our finance statement. In a week or two we will be sending out a detailed financial statement for the past fiscal year. I have said this before, but perhaps I should say it again that the cost for the Church windows is coming out of our reserve. This was decided a couple of years ago when we realized it had to be done. So the cost of the windows is not the reason we've come out in the red this year.

I am going to ask for help in three ways. 1) As I look at our finances I believe we will come out okay this fiscal year if everyone raises their contribution by 10%. I know not everyone can, but if you can't, could you help us out a little bit more than what you give at present. I know you will be blessed and I bet you won't miss anything extra that you give. Remember, God will not let anyone get ahead of him in being generous. 2) I would ask if you would be willing to do direct deposit; that would be especially appreciated because that way you would be giving to the parish even if you are unable to come. 3) I ask our parishioners to remember us in their will. That has been a big help to us over the years.

Before I conclude I want to offer just a couple of brief thoughts. Let us consider the value of one dollar. Some people still tell themselves a dollar a week was good enough for my grandfather, so it's good enough for me. In some cases I know it's all a person can afford. But I want to remind people, in case they haven't noticed, the dollar is worth only a tiny fraction of what it was worth in grandfather's time. It has slipped considerably in value in just the past few years. I have decided to give back half of my salary before the end of the year. I'm not saying this for praise or pity, but simple to assure you that if I ask you to sacrifice, I am willing to also.

We need your help so that we can continue to serve you. Remember the pastor who told his parishioners: "I have good news and bad news. The good news is that we have all the money we need. The bad news is, it's in your pockets." Amen.

All Saints
November 1, 2009

INTRODUCTION – (Rev. 7:2-4, 9-14; 1 John 3:1-3; Mt. 5:1-12a) Our first reading is from the book of Revelation. The section just preceding today's passage describes the end of the world. The sun will become dark and the moon will become red as blood and there will be a great earthquake all over the earth. People will try to hide from all these terrible things and they will ask: "Who can survive?" Today's reading is the answer to that question - those will survive who have followed Christ faithfully. The number 144,000 is a symbolic number, symbolizing perfection. Notice after it refers to the 144,000 it speaks of those who are saved as such a large crowd that no one can count them.

HOMILY – I am part of our parish book club and a few months ago Thomas Merton's *Seven Storey Mountain* was chosen as the book we would read. I totally *loved* the book and since then have read three other books about or by Thomas Merton and have begun reading a few others. To say the least, I was greatly impressed by him. There is a passage from *Seven Storey Mountain* I would like to read to you. At this point in Merton's life he was a new Catholic, not yet six months away from having been baptized. He is with his friend Robert Lax. Let me read it in Merton's own words.

They were walking down Sixth Avenue one evening when Lax asked Merton: "What do you want to be, anyway?" In Merton's own words: I could not say, "I want to be Thomas Merton the well-known writer of all those book reviews in the back pages of the Times Book Review," or " Thomas Merton the assistant instructor of Freshman-English at the New Life Social Institute for Progress and Culture," so I put the thing on the spiritual plane, where I knew it belonged and said: "I don't know; I guess what I want is to be a good Catholic." "What do you mean, you want to be a good Catholic?" The explanation I gave was lame enough, and expressed my confusion, and betrayed how little I had really thought about it at all. Lax did not accept it. "What you should say" – he told me - "what you should say is that you want to be a saint." A saint! The thought struck me as a little weird. I said: "how do you expect me to become a saint?" "By wanting to," said Lax, simply. "I can't be a saint," I said, "I can't be a saint." And my mind darkened with a confusion of realities and unrealities: the knowledge of my own sins, and the false humility which makes men say that they cannot do the things that they must do, cannot reach the level that they must reach: the cowardice that says: "I am satisfied to save my soul, to keep out of mortal sin," but which means, by those words: "I do not want to give up my sins and my attachments." But Lax said: "No. All that is necessary to be a saint is to want to be one. Don't you believe that God will make you what He created you to be, if you will consent to let Him do it?" (pg. 260)

Thomas Merton became convinced that Robert Lax was right. We were created to become saints, but it is something we must want to become. He also came to realize we cannot make ourselves saints. We can only open ourselves to the holiness of God – for God alone is holy. As he says 11 years later in his book *The Sign of Jonas* (pg 162): "A saint is not so much a man who realizes that he possesses virtues and sanctity as one who is overwhelmed by the sanctity of God." We become holy by "sharing in his being" and "rising above the level of everything that is not God."

Sharing in God's being is the same as the concept frequently used in Scripture, especially in St. John's gospel. It is the idea of sharing in his life, which comes to us through the sacraments. Saint John tells us today: "See what love the Father has bestowed on us that we may be called the children of God. Yet that is what we are."

The term "saint" is often used in the New Testament to refer to Christians in general, for they who share God's life are holy (that's what "saint" means). Very early on it was used to designate people whose holiness was outstanding, especially the martyrs. Today the official list of saints' names is close to 7000 people whose holiness the Church officially recognizes. They give us heroic examples of having faithfully followed Christ. We all have heroes, especially as we grow up. It's good to have people as heroes, people who excel in living holy lives and not just sports figures or rock stars. It's good also to have friends in high places when we need help. We often ask our friends to pray for us in difficult times, why not ask those whom we know are special friends of God. We don't adore saints (as we are sometimes accused of doing), we adore only God, but we also honor the saints' holy lives and ask for their prayers.

Today we honor all those who haven't made it to the major leagues of sainthood, parents, grandparents, friends who have inspired us and helped us along our journey to God. They are part of "that great multitude which no one could count, from every nation, race, people and tongue" which our first reading from Revelation told us about today. We ask their prayers, we ask them to help us to someday be with them as saints to enjoy the holiness and glory for which God created us. Amen.

All Souls

November 2, 2008

INTRODUCTION – (2 Maccabees 12:43-46; Romans 5:5-11; John 6:37-40) Our first reading, from the book of Maccabees, comes from about 100 years before Christ. At that time in history the Greeks were the dominant power and they were trying to get the Jews to abandon their faith and follow the beliefs of the pagans. Those who would not give in were persecuted and put to death. The loyal Jews fought back. In one of their battles, many Jews were killed. As they were being buried, it was found that they had small statues of pagan gods attached to their garments. These Jews were loyal to their Jewish beliefs, but they had, to some extent, given in to paganism. Just in case those pagan gods were real, they were carrying with them statues of pagan gods to give them protection. Their leader, Judas Maccabeus, took up a collection to send to Jerusalem for sacrifices to be offered up to the Lord for those people. He believed their hearts were, in general, in the right place, but for the weakness in their faith they had to be forgiven. In this piece of history from 100 B.C., we can see the beginnings of the belief that our prayers can help those who have died, a belief that is still part of our faith.

HOMILY – Praying for our deceased relatives and friends is what our feast of All Souls is about today. However, I had the hardest time getting started with today's homily. I kept putting it off. It's not as if I do not believe in praying for friends and relatives who have died. I do it all the time and it has been a tradition in the Church from the beginning, and even before that as we heard in our first reading.

I think the difficulty I had in developing my homily comes from two sources. First, many people don't like to hear about death and what might come afterwards. We know we can't avoid it, but my sense is that many people believe that if they don't think about it, it won't happen, at least not for a long time. My suspicion is that my father was that way. I constantly tried to get him to make a will but he never did. As a CPA he would have known it was a good idea. I think making a will would have made the prospect of his own death too concrete and too real for him to deal with.

The second reason today's homily was hard was that I would have to talk about Purgatory. It's an idea that many Christians deny. I remember once I was helping a family prepare the liturgy for their deceased father and they insisted "absolutely no mention of Purgatory." It's as if it were a bad word. They wanted to think their father was perfect, I guess, and was already in heaven. Most of us would like to believe that our loved ones go straight to heaven when they die – period. If this were true, then they would not need our prayers. If they went to the other place, God forbid, our prayers would do them no good. The Church teaches, in every Mass we have for a person who died and in today's feast, that our prayers do help our relatives and friends who have left this world as they journey to eternal life.

Purgatory, among all the mysteries and beliefs of the Church is an extremely logical and comforting doctrine. It's logical if we ask ourselves how many of us think we will be perfect when we die. There may even be some who are perfect right now. I would ask them to identify themselves, but if they're perfect, they will also be too humble to do so. Even those who lived a good life may still have a little room for improvement, they may still not love God or others quite enough. That's where Purgatory comes in – it's an opportunity to grow into the most loving, most holy person we can possibly be. As a result we would then be filled with God's peace and joy and love to the fullest extent. Luther rejected the idea of Purgatory because of the abuse of indulgences at the time. Today, the concept of Purgatory has been rejected by many because of all the negative images of suffering and punishment that we grew up with. Actually, I think for the souls in Purgatory, happiness far outweighs the unhappiness. Their salvation is sure, they are more closely united with God than they had ever experienced before in their lives, they are on their way to the enjoyment of God's kingdom in the fullest possible way. But they're not there yet and that's the painful part.

If you read the book, "*The Five People You Meet in Heaven*," I think you get a good, practical image of Purgatory. It's not a religious book, it's very entertaining and it pictured for me what Purgatory might be like as we work out issues, regrets, hurts, conflicts, etc., that we might take with us when we die.

To demonstrate that Purgatory makes so much sense, I think that those who deny Purgatory have had to find a substitute for it in their thinking about the next life. For many that substitute is reincarnation. In reincarnation a person supposedly keeps working for greater and greater purity and holiness until they are ready to be perfectly one with God. However, reincarnation comes from Hinduism. Actually a Hindu does not look forward to reincarnation because they don't want to have to pass through this world of pain and suffering one more time. I suspect the notion of reincarnation has been adopted by many Westerners, even Christians, because it fits our culture of "buy now, pay later." They figure they can live any way they want and can postpone having to pay any consequences. Our faith tells us, "now is the acceptable time, now is the day of salvation." God gives us what we need in this life to help us know him and serve him in this life. If we do not do it perfectly, Purgatory is there to finish the job. Today, we renew our faith in life after death. Today too we renew our belief in the power of prayer to help our loved ones, even those who are no longer among us, for in Christ they are still one with us. With Christ our great high priest, we offer now the greatest prayer there is, the Eucharist.

31st Sunday in Ordinary Time
November 5, 2006

(Dt. 6:2-6; Hebrews 7:23-28; Mark 12:28b-34) The rabbis and Jewish religious leaders at the time of Jesus would often discuss which of their 613 laws was the most important. They asked Jesus' opinion and as usual Jesus got right to the heart of the matter. Jesus was not saying the others do not count or are unimportant. He was saying that love is the spirit behind all of them. If we follow the command of love, we will keep the others, if we keep the others without love we are legalists or as Paul says in his famous 13th chapter of 1 Corinthians "If I have not love, I am nothing." Jesus was asked for one commandment, but he gave us two, to show that the two are inseparable. Part of the problems people have in today's world is that they have forgotten the first part of this commandment. That's why they have problems with the second. It's interesting too to notice the word "commandment." It reminds us that we don't always feel love for God or for others, but we are obliged to do it anyway if we are going to fulfill our highest potential as a human being and if we are going to please God.

I was going to bring with me today all the books I have that have the word "love" in the title. But there were too many to bring. So, just think of a big stack of books up here. My purpose in mentioning there are so many books is to illustrate that love can be very complex and learning to love God and others is not always as easy as we would like to think that it is. In is interesting that the English language, which has a plentitude of words, relies so heavily on the one word "love" to mean so many things. Even the Greek language, which was rather primitive, had three words for the word love, depending on the kind of love that was being spoken of. We use the one word "love" to describe everything from a score in tennis to the most selfish, lustful cravings to the most sublime and unselfish act of kindness toward another. For this reason it is a challenge to talk about and a challenge to put into practice.

The biggest misconception about love in today's world is to equate it with feelings. Too many people think love means having nice warm, friendly feelings toward someone. Well, it is and it isn't. Love is an emotion, but the kind of love Jesus is talking about is much more. Warm feelings don't always feed the hungry or help a person in need. Love is not primarily something vague, fuzzy and warm. Love is a matter of what one does rather than what one feels.

One of the Peanuts' cartoons had Linus telling his sister Lucy that he wanted to be a doctor when he grew up. Lucy responded in her usual cynical fashion by saying "You, a doctor? That's a laugh. You know why you couldn't be a doctor? Because you don't love humankind." Linus thought about this for a moment then said "I do love humankind. It's people I can't stand." It's easy to have nice warm, happy feelings of love for vague humanity, or even for a God who will do for us whatever we want him to do. But where are those nice warm happy feelings when a parent has to get up in the middle of the night to care for a crying baby or when an adult child has to care for an aging parent or even when God commands things we don't want to do. When we do the right thing, that's love at work also.

There is a beautiful story in *Chicken Soup for the Soul* about a little girl who was dying of a very rare disease. Her only hope for survival was to get a blood transfusion from her five year old brother who had survived the same disease and whose body had developed antibodies needed to combat the illness. The doctor explained to the little boy what a transfusion was and asked if he would be willing to give blood to his sister. He hesitated for a moment then said "yes, if it will save Lisa." As the transfusion progressed he lay in bed next to his sister and smiled, along with all the medical staff, as they saw color return to Lisa's cheeks. Then the little boy's smile faded and with a very serious look on his face and a trembling voice he asked the doctor "Will I start to die now?" The boy had misunderstood the doctor and thought he would have to give his sister all his blood. Love is not always a happy, painless, easy, carefree thing. Love, when it is real love, requires unselfishness and that's not always easy, especially when it is required of us over long periods of time.

Love has some difficult elements to it such as sacrifice and unselfishness. You know, when we are born we're pretty self centered creatures. We know when we're hungry, when we're in pain, when we're tired and we don't mind letting the whole world know about it. That's OK for a baby. But we're supposed to grow out of that stage and realize we're not the center of the universe. When we grow in love we are learning to reach out to others and this is a sign of maturity.

A word about love for God. Feelings enter in here too and when they're not present people become confused. When they don't get good feelings from prayer or Mass they often feel they are losing their faith or God has abandoned them or they just quit trying. Sometimes our love for God produces good feelings, but love for God is not measured by how we feel. Basically, love for God is a matter of giving God our trust, our time and our obedience. Jesus gave us a reliable measure of our love for God when he told us: "If you love me you will keep my commandments."

We come together today to offer God our worship and our love. As we recall Jesus unselfish love for us in giving his life for us on the cross, we ask him to help us learn the true meaning of love. Amen.

32nd Sunday in Ordinary Time

November 8, 2009

INTRODUCTION – (1 Kings 17:10-16; Hebrews 9:24-28; Mark 12:38-44) I want to begin by saying something about the second reading. The author of the Letter to the Hebrews was interested in showing the superiority of Jesus' sacrifice to those of the Old Testament. He is referring especially to the once a year sacrifice on the Day of Atonement (Yom Kippur) as was celebrated just six weeks ago on Sept 27. In the time before 70 AD when the Romans destroyed the Temple, the High Priest alone would enter the Holy Place. Year after year he would offer sacrifice for the sins of God's people. The Letter to the Hebrews emphasizes that Christ's sacrifice for sins took place only once and didn't need to be offered again and again because his sacrifice was perfect. We participate in this perfect sacrifice of Christ each time we come to Mass.

Our first reading will make more sense if we know that the events that are described in the reading happened during a severe famine. We have to marvel at the faith of this widow.

HOMILY – Two weeks ago I asked our parishioners to raise their contributions by 10% or by however much they could afford. Last Sunday's collection was very impressive – it was over $10,000. I know there were a couple of unusually large checks that accounted for that amount. I see this as a sign that most parishioners heard my message and are responding. That's good and I thank you very much. I know not all of our parishioners were here two weeks ago when I gave my money talk, so this week I sent out my homily to everyone I could who comes here because I'm asking for everyone's help. So if you have received that homily, don't think I'm badgering you. I'm just trying to communicate with all the people who help support us. I'll dispense you from reading the homily if you heard it the first time two weeks ago.

It's just a coincidence that our gospel is about money today. The most obvious part of the gospel is the contrast between the people who made big donations (which would have made a noticeable amount of noise with all the large coins clinking in the donation boxes) and the tiny donation from the poor widow. A few years ago someone gave me a widow's mite. I was going to show it to you but you wouldn't have been able to see it from the pews. I don't think it's even half the size of a penny. Whenever I read this story in the past, I always assumed that Jesus was condemning those who were showy about their generosity and he was praising the poor widow and expecting us to follow her example. Maybe praise of this woman is implicit in his remark, but notice Jesus didn't really expand on what he observed. He could have been thinking this woman was generous in the extreme and she would be greatly blessed like the woman in our first reading who gave her last morsel of food to the prophet.

He could have been thinking maybe she should have been more practical and should have saved her two copper coins for something to eat. He could have been referring to his remark about the scribes who devoured the savings of widows. Or he could have been thinking of his own sacrifice (giving his life in love for us) that was soon to take place. He didn't say what he was thinking. Let us be clear about this: he wasn't condemning giving large amounts to charity. He was practical and knew bills had to be paid. After all, St. Paul tells us God loves a cheerful giver. We don't even know if this poor woman was cheerful or not cheerful. We only know she gave more than all the rest if you consider she gave all she had. I would like to speculate there were people who gave large sums of money who were not necessarily looking for human praise or respect. They were simply trying to give honor and glory to God and to the worship of God. Certainly Jesus would have approved their generosity. I would speculate further that there were people who could afford to give a lot more than they did, but they gave very little. Without much commentary from Jesus, I don't know if today's gospel tells us much about money. But it does tell us about something else: our judgment about things is not always the way God sees things. Our gospel tells us we can observe what a person does but only God can see into our hearts. "As high as the heavens are above the earth, so high are my ways above your ways and my thoughts above your thoughts," says the Lord. (Isaiah 55:9) Who could have known this woman gave away everything she had just by watching her. Who would have known she didn't have a pot of gold hidden under her bed? Only Jesus could have known. Only Jesus knows what's in our hearts, Sometimes we don't even know ourselves what's in our hearts. How many times have we asked ourselves:

"why did I do that?" "Why did I say such and such to that person?" "Why do I feel the way that I do?" We can only judge what people do. If they are hurting us or someone else, or if they're being dishonest, for example, we can condemn their actions. Some people have the responsibility to do so - like parents or judges or police personnel, etc. We may even try to guess a person's motivation, but only God can and does see into our hearts. My mother used to always tell me, "even if I don't see you, God sees you." I think if more people were conscious of this, we would have a kinder world. That's one message I do get from today's gospel.

Now that I'm on the topic of money, I want to say something about gambling. This is so elementary I hesitate to say it, but I'm saying it anyway. Gambling is big business and the ones who make the big money from it, after much perseverance, got Ohioans to approve gambling in our state. The Church does not condemn gambling itself, but it can be done irresponsibly. If you decide to gamble, don't gamble more than you can afford to lose, because eventually you will. That's how the people who own the casinos get rich. Think of gambling as a form of entertainment, but if you're gambling more than you can afford to lose, then it's become an addiction. If you're spending money at the casinos, don't forget to set some aside for charity. If you neglect charity so you can splurge more on being entertained, that's not right either. Those are my words about gambling now that it will be in our backyard. God knows what's in our hearts all the time, even the way we spend our money. It tells a lot about our priorities. By the way, giving to charity is like gambling. We are betting on God's generosity and that he will bless us. That's a sure bet. The only part of that gamble we don't know is when it will pay off. Amen.

33rd Sunday in Ordinary Time
November 15, 2009

INTRODUCTION – (Daniel 12:1-3; Heb 10:11-14; Mk 13:24-32) The Greek text of the Book of Revelation begins with the word "apocalypsis." The word means revealing something or making something fully known. Thus the book is called the "Apocalypse" or "Revelation" which is simply a translation of the Greek word. There are, however, many passages in the Bible that are apocalyptic in nature. Usually they were written during a time when God's people were being persecuted. They gave hope to God's people during those times, hope that if they remained faithful to God they would be victorious in the end. Our first reading today, from the Book of Daniel, written about 165 BC, is an example of apocalyptic writing. It was a time of Jewish persecution. Preceding today's reading the Book of Daniel describes several visions Daniel had about the immediate future of God's people. The vision predicted this time would be "unsurpassed in distress" when the Syrians were trying to obliterate faithful Jews and the faith of the Jews. Today's passage predicts the Archangel Michael, the guardian of the Jews, would come to the aid of God's people. The passage contains a clear belief in resurrection to glory for those who remained faithful and a resurrection to ignominy for those who had not.

HOMILY – I recently read (the Joyful Noiseletter, January, 2010, pg 2) about a woman who left instructions for her children that when she died they should place on her grave a parking meter that read: "Time Expired." Even in the face of death, she was obviously a lady with a good sense of humor.

As we rapidly approach the end of the liturgical year, "Time Expired" is also the theme of today's liturgy. Our liturgical year began in Advent and it ends right before another Advent begins in two weeks. Shortly after Advent and Christmas, we will see the end of 2009 and begin a new calendar year. As another year rapidly comes to an end, we are reminded that eventually all things will come to an end and eternity will begin.

Let me first focus on the end of time, then I will say something about what comes after that. Our gospel today describes the end of this world as we know it. The sun and moon and stars by which we mark the days and months and seasons of the year will disappear. Because this traumatic event was being described in a way that people 2000 years ago could understand, we do not know if the end of this world will happen exactly as the gospel describes it. I'm sure we've all seen our share of movies that pictured other ways in which our world might come to an end, such as being taken over by apes or by regenerated dinosaurs, or it could end by colliding with an asteroid from outer space or by an invasion of aliens from Mars or some distant galaxy, or more realistically, it could end by a nuclear world war or by a germ that could not be stopped. In all these movies, the world really never ends. It seems there is always a superhero who somehow stops the catastrophe from happening. Today's gospel does not tell us there is any superhero who will keep the world from ending, for it will end. But there is One, a super- superhero who will bring a new creation into being. This new creation will not be like the present world with suffering and pain and time expiring, but it will be a world of everlasting peace and joy, founded on love for God and for one another.

We don't like to think about time expiring and the end of all things. Our good and loving Lord reminds us of those things because he knows that only those who have learned how to love in this life will be able to participate in the new creation that is built on love. Again and again our Lord reminds us that the choices we make in this life will determine what is ahead for us in the next. Our culture today believes somehow everyone will end up happy in God's kingdom. I wish that were so, but if it were to be that everyone ends up happy in God's kingdom, why would Jesus have gone through so much in order to tell us it is important how we live our life now?

Before concluding, there is one verse in today's gospel that is confusing: when Jesus says: "This generation will not pass away until all these things have taken place."

The last thing Jesus tells us in today's gospel is that no one, not even Jesus, knows when all this will take place or when he will return again to raise the dead back to life and to initiate the reign of God and his eternal kingdom. However, when he says: "This generation will not pass away…," he seems to be predicting what he tells us is unpredictable. Fr. Vawter, in his commentary on The Four Gospels, states that these passages about the end of time seem to be compiled from things that Jesus said on a number of occasions. Some of these verses may have been taken out of their original historical context. This particular verse, that "this generation will not pass away…," may have been spoken by Jesus on another occasion, such as when he predicted the destruction of the Temple. It could have ended up being placed here because the early Church expected Jesus was going to return for the final judgment in the very near future. It took several decades before the first Christians finally realized Jesus' second coming was not going to happen immediately and by then the gospels were written. That interpretation makes sense to me.

Not knowing when all these things may happen are not meant to frighten a person, unless they need to be frightened into living a good life, but it should motivate us to be prepared. It should give us hope during any type of trial that our time and trial "now" is temporary, but "eternity" is forever. Amen.

Christ the King

November 22, 2009

INTRODUCTION – (Daniel 7:13-14; Rev 1:5-8; John 18:33-37) Again this week we hear from the book of Daniel, a book that was written during a time when the Jews were suffering a terrible persecution for their faith. Today's reading describes how God would triumph in the end. God would establish a kingdom that would be everlasting. God is here described as "the Ancient One." His kingdom would be ruled by one who is described as "like a son of man." God would give this "son of man" dominion, glory and kingship. The term "son of man" simply means a human being, but today's passage invests the term with new depth and mystery. You might recall, "son of man" was the favorite term Jesus used to describe himself.

HOMILY – There was a priest who was giving his homily using many gestures. With one grand gesture, he accidentally swept his homily notes off the podium and onto the floor. After he picked them up and tried to reassemble them, the congregation heard him say to himself: "Now, where was I?" One member of the congregation answered back: "Right near the end!"

That has no connection with my homily today, except I hope it never happens to me, but I thought it was funny. Today we celebrate Christ as our King. He's not like any other king we have heard about as we studied history. His kingdom does not belong to this world. He does not force us to serve him; he only asks us to love him. He does not parade in gold and royal robes; he doesn't need to. All creation belongs to him – except for those human hearts who choose not to surrender their love – and it will be to their loss unless they do. All other kings must eventually lay aside their power and return to their creator for their power is temporary, but Jesus' kingdom is an everlasting dominion that shall not be taken away; his kingship shall not be destroyed. But as a king, we are reminded that we owe Jesus our homage, our obedience, and our thanks. It is on this theme of thanks that I wish to continue my homily.

Even our nation gives thanks this week. Those who have faith and who honor Christ as king know that giving thanks needs to be offered more than once a year. Actually giving thanks is central to our faith, as St. Paul wrote to the Galatians (3:15): "dedicate yourselves to thankfulness sing gratefully to God from your hearts in psalms, hymns, and inspired songs. Whatever you do, whether in speech or in action, do it in the name of the Lord Jesus. Give thanks to God the Father through him." It is our faith tradition that as a minimum, based on the Commandments, we give thanks at least once a week – on the Lord's day.

We all get lots of things in our emails I'm sure. This past week I received an email about a man who dreamed he died and went to heaven. When he arrived, St. Peter gave the man's guardian angel the assignment to show this newcomer around. So the angel took him into a very large building three stories high. They walked in the front door and there on the first floor were hundreds of angels working feverishly, flitting around with papers and note pads and cell phones, writing down messages and phone calls, etc. His angel explained this is the Receiving Section where prayers and requests are processed from all over the world. Then his angel took him up to the second floor where there were hundreds of angels busy filling large envelopes and boxes and sending them off. This, the angel explained, is the Packaging and Delivery Section where favors and blessings and answers to prayers were sent out. Finally they came to the third floor, which was mostly empty except for one angel who was sitting idly at a table reading a magazine, waiting patiently for a phone call or a message from somewhere. This was the Acknowledgement Section where people reply to favors received. The man asked his angel how does a person acknowledge a favor or a blessing and the angel answered, "It's simple. They just say 'Thank you, Lord.'"

In the Friday's Enquirer on page 13 there was an article reporting that UNICEF claims that one billion children in today's world are deprived of food, shelter, clean water or health care and hundreds of millions more are threatened by violence. Nearly 200 million youngsters are chronically malnourished, more than 140 million are forced to work, and millions of girls and boys of all ages are subjected to sexual violence. More than 24,000 children under the age of five die every day from preventable causes like pneumonia, malaria, measles and malnutrition. Grim statistics we don't like to hear (that's probably why the article was buried on page 13). I don't like to think about them either and I'm not trying to make anyone feel guilty because they happened to have been born in this country rather than in a third world country. I'm just trying to encourage people to stop and think this week that if we have food in the refrigerator, clothes to wear, a roof overhead and a place to sleep; if we woke up this morning with more health than illness; if we have never experienced the fear of battle, the loneliness of imprisonment, the agony of torture or the pangs of starvation; if we have a place to worship without the fear of harassment, arrest or torture; if we know how to read;

we are more blessed than millions and billions of people in the world today. If we are so blessed, we must say "Thank you Lord" over and over, but we must also, however we can and when the opportunity arises, share some of our blessings with those not so blessed, even if all we can do is sincerely pray for them. May you find a way to truly give thanks this Thursday and may this holiday be also a holy day to reinforce in you the importance of a grateful heart. Amen.

Third Sunday of Easter – A Cycle

May 8, 2011

Delivered at the 50th Wedding Anniversary Mass at St. Peter in Chains Cathedral

HOMILY – (Acts 2:14, 22-33; 1 Peter 1:17-21; Luke 24:13-35) I am honored to celebrate with you today. I'm Fr. Joe Robinson, pastor of St. Boniface Church. I am also the dean of the Cathedral Deanery and it was because I am dean that I originally thought that's why I was invited to preside at today's liturgy. But the idea did cross my mind that since I have been ordained for 47 years, maybe I was asked to come because I'm about as old as everyone else here. That way you all would feel more comfortable. Maybe with a little luck and God's blessing, I'll make it to my 50th anniversary in a few years. A 50th anniversary is something worth celebrating and something worth giving thanks for that is what we are doing here today.

I have three little stories you might enjoy (all three are from *Reader's Digest: Laughter, the Best Medicine*, pgs. 154, 163 & 175): 1) A lady was telling her friend that after she and her husband had a huge argument, they ended up not talking to each other. Finally, on the third day, he asked where one of his shirts was. "Oh," she said, "now you are speaking to me." He was confused and asked: "What are you talking about?" "Haven't you noticed I haven't spoken to you for three days?" she asked. "No," he said. "I just thought we were getting along."

2) A lady and her sister in law were discussing how long they've been married. The sister-in-law commented: "you've been married to my brother for 50 years. That's a long time." "A long, long time" she agreed. Then she smiled and said: "you know the strangest idea occurred to me the other day. If I had killed your brother the first time I felt like it, I'd be out of jail by now."

3) A husband and wife were comparing notes one day. She pointed out to him, "I have a higher IQ, did better on my SAT's and made more money than you." "Yeah," he said. "But when you look at the big picture, I'm still way ahead of you." Puzzled she asked: "How do you figure?" "I married better," he replied.

So, in the name of the Church, in the name of the sacredness of the sacrament of marriage, I thank you for your 50 years of dedication and love for each other. I thank you for doing more than just silently getting along and for not killing one another when you felt like it. I hope today that you each feel deep in your heart that you got the better part of the deal when you got married.

Leonard Pitts, whose editorials appear in the Enquirer, wrote one a week ago that was inspired by the marriage of Prince William and Kate Middleton. I am going to steal some of his ideas, ideas that are profound, ideas that will not surprise any of you but are always worth remembering. He said marriage is an act of faith. It is a willingness to make a bet that it's possible to love someone always and forever. As you all know, loving each other always and forever is not just romance. It is as much a function of commitment and work as it is a function of love. The capacity and willingness to make that bet, to put in the required work, to be faithful to a commitment, are slowly disappearing from American life. Fifty years ago 70 percent of all American adults were married. Now it's about 54 percent. As so many marriages end in disaster, for a numerous reasons, marriage in this day and age is an act of hope as well as an act of faith. It is an act of defiance against cynicism and pessimism. St. Paul has given us one of the best descriptions there is of love when he tells us it patient and kind, it is not jealous or snobbish or rude or self-

seeking, not prone to anger or holding grudges. There is no limit to its forbearance, its trust, its hope, its power to endure. If people have that kind of love, no wonder Paul can say, "love never fails."

Our gospel today presents us with the picture of Jesus' frightened and frustrated disciples. This wasn't the first time they were frightened or frustrated by our Lord nor was it the last time. The kingdom he came to offer would be much greater than they were capable of imagining. The way into that kingdom would be the cross. Through good times and bad, he never abandoned them even when they deserted him. In our journey through life sometimes things can get pretty discouraging. Things don't always happen the way we think they should and we feel anger, discouragement and sadness. Through good times and bad, our Lord is with us, although we do not always recognize him. He has won victory for us over all those forces that seek to pull us down. He has declared victory even over our ultimate enemy - sin and death. It is that victory that we celebrate especially during this Easter season. All through the year Jesus is with us, teaching us with his word in the Scriptures and nourishing us with the bread of his own flesh and blood as he does today.

Again I congratulate you and thank you for overcoming the challenges and fears and discouragements we all face at times throughout our lives. I congratulate you and thank you for your patience, your many sacrifices, your sensitivity to one another, your care and concern, your enduring love. May you trust in our Lord's presence with you and always experience hope and joy and a love that never fails. Amen.

718
601
508
738

A Priest Is a Gift from God

by Rita Ring

C F G
Come My chil - dren to My al - tar, A
Come My chil - dren to My al - tar, A
VERSE 2
C F C
to Refrain
C F G
priest is a gift from God. 2. Come to Me, My lit - tle chil-dren,
priest is a gift from God.
C F G C F G
I want to pos-sess your soul. Give your hearts to Je-sus and Mar - y,
C F G C F C
You will be one in Our Hearts, A priest is a gift from God.
F G C F C
Of - fer sac - ri - fice My chil-dren, A priest is a gift from God.
F G C F G
One in your heart, one in your mind, one in this ho - ly ban-quet,
C F G C F C
to Refrain
Come My chil-dren to My al-tar, A priest is a gift from God.

How to Become a Shepherd of Christ Associate

The Shepherds of Christ has prayer chapters all over the world praying for the priests, the Church and the world. These prayers that Father Carter compiled in the summer of 1994 began this worldwide network of prayer. Currently the prayers are in eight languages with the Church's *Imprimatur*. Fr. Carter had the approval of his Jesuit provincial for this movement, writing the Newsletter every 2 months for 6 1/2 years. After his death, and with his direction, we in the Shepherds of Christ circulated the *Priestly Newsletter Book II* to 95,000 priests with other writings. We have prayed daily for the priests, the Church, and the world since 1994. Associates are called to join prayer Chapters and help us circulate this newsletter centered on spreading devotion to the Sacred Heart and Immaculate Heart and helping to renew the Church through greater holiness. Please form a Prayer Chapter & order a Prayer Manual.

Apostles of the Eucharistic Heart of Jesus

The Shepherds of Christ have people dedicated to spending two hours weekly before the Blessed Sacrament in the Tabernacle. They pray for the following intentions:

1) For the spread of the devotion to the Hearts of Jesus and Mary culminating in the reign of the Sacred Heart and the triumph of the Immaculate Heart.
2) For the Pope.
3) For all bishops of the world.
4) For all priests.
5) For all sisters and brothers in religious life.
6) For all members of the Shepherds of Christ Movement, and for the spread of this movement to the world.
7) For all members of the Catholic Church.
8) For all members of the human family.
9) For all souls in purgatory.

This movement, ***Apostles of the Eucharistic Heart of Jesus***, was began with Fr. Carter. Please inquire. Shepherds of Christ Ministries P.O. Box 627, China, Indiana 47250 USA or 1-888-211-3041 or info@sofc.org

Prayer for Union with Jesus

Come to me, Lord, and possess my soul. Come into my heart and permeate my soul. Help me to sit in silence with You and let You work in my heart.

I am Yours to possess. I am Yours to use. I want to be selfless and only exist in You. Help me to spoon out all that is me and be an empty vessel ready to be filled by You. Help me to die to myself and live only for You. Use me as You will. Let me never draw my attention back to myself. I only want to operate as You do, dwelling within me.

I am Yours, Lord. I want to have my life in You. I want to do the will of the Father. Give me the strength to put aside the world and let You operate my very being. Help me to act as You desire. Strengthen me against the distractions of the devil to take me from Your work.

When I worry, I have taken my focus off of You and placed it on myself. Help me not to give in to the promptings of others to change what in my heart You are making very clear to me. I worship You, I adore You and I love You. Come and dwell in me now.

Written by Rita Robinson Ring

Prayer Before the Holy Sacrifice of the Mass

Let me be a holy sacrifice and unite with God in the sacrament of His greatest love.

I want to be one in Him in this act of love, where He gives Himself to me and I give myself as a sacrifice to Him. Let me be a holy sacrifice as I become one with Him in this my act of greatest love to Him.

Let me unite with Him more, that I may more deeply love Him. May I help make reparation to His adorable Heart and the heart of His Mother, Mary. With greatest love, I offer myself to You and pray that You will accept my sacrifice of greatest love. I give myself to You and unite in Your gift of Yourself to me. Come and possess my soul.

Cleanse me, strengthen me, heal me. Dear Holy Spirit act in the heart of Mary to make me more and more like Jesus.

Father, I offer this my sacrifice, myself united to Jesus in the Holy Spirit to You. Help me to love God more deeply in this act of my greatest love.

Give me the grace to grow in my knowledge, love and service of You and for this to be my greatest participation in the Mass. Give me the greatest graces to love You so deeply in this Mass, You who are so worthy of my love.

Written by Rita Robinson Ring

Father Carter requested that these be prayed in prayer chapters all over the world.

Shepherds of Christ Associates

PRAYER MANUAL

Shepherds of Christ Publications
China, Indiana

Shepherds of Christ Prayers

Imprimi Potest: Rev. Bradley M. Schaeffer, S.J.
Provincial
Chicago Province, The Society of Jesus

Imprimatur: Most Rev. Carl K. Moeddel
Auxiliary Bishop
Archdiocese of Cincinnati

The Shepherds of Christ Associates Prayer Manual is published by Shepherds of Christ Publications, an arm of Shepherds of Christ Ministries, P.O. Box 627 China, Indiana 47250 USA.

Founder, Shepherds of Christ Ministries:
Father Edward J. Carter, S.J.

For more information contact:
Shepherds of Christ Associates
P.O. Box 627
China, Indiana 47250- USA
Tel. 812-273-8405
Toll Free: 1-888-211-3041
Fax 812-273-3182

Chapter Meeting Prayer Format

The prayer format below should be followed at chapter meetings of *Shepherds of Christ Associates*. All prayers, not just those said specifically for priests, should include the intention of praying for all the needs of priests the world over.

1. **Hymns.** Hymns may be sung at any point of the prayer part of the meeting.

2. **Holy Spirit Prayer.** Come, Holy Spirit, almighty Sanctifier, God of love, who filled the Virgin Mary with grace, who wonderfully changed the hearts of the apostles, who endowed all Your martyrs with miraculous courage, come and sanctify us. Enlighten our minds, strengthen our wills, purify our consciences, rectify our judgment, set our hearts on fire, and preserve us from the misfortunes of resisting Your inspirations. Amen.

3. **The Rosary.**

4. **Salve Regina.** "Hail Holy Queen, Mother of mercy, our life, our sweetness, and our hope. To you do we cry, poor banished children of Eve. To you do we send up our sighs, our mourning, our weeping in this vale of tears. Turn, then, most gracious advocate, your eyes of mercy toward us and after this, our exile, show unto us the blessed fruit of your womb, Jesus, O clement, O loving, O sweet Virgin Mary. Amen."

5. **The Memorare.** "Remember, O most gracious Virgin Mary, that never was it known that anyone who fled to your protection, implored your help, or sought your intercession was left unaided. Inspired by this confidence, I fly unto you, O Virgin of virgins, my Mother. To you I come, before you I stand, sinful and

sorrowful. O Mother of the Word Incarnate, despise not my petitions, but, in your mercy, hear and answer me. Amen."

6. **Seven Hail Marys in honor of the Seven Sorrows of Mary.** Mary has promised very special graces to those who do this on a daily basis. Included in the promises of Our Lady for those who practice this devotion is her pledge to give special assistance at the hour of death, including the sight of her face. The seven sorrows are:

(1) The first sorrow: the prophecy of Simeon (Hail Mary).
(2) The second sorrow: the flight into Egypt (Hail Mary).
(3) The third sorrow: the loss of the Child Jesus in the temple (Hail Mary).
(4) The fourth sorrow: Jesus and Mary meet on the way to the cross (Hail Mary).
(5) The fifth sorrow: Jesus dies on the cross (Hail Mary).
(6) The sixth sorrow: Jesus is taken down from the cross and laid in Mary's arms (Hail Mary).
(7) The seventh sorrow: the burial of Jesus (Hail Mary).

7. **Litany of the Blessed Virgin Mary.**

Lord, have mercy on us.
Christ, have mercy on us.
Lord, have mercy on us. Christ, hear us.
Christ, graciously hear us.
God, the Father of heaven, *have mercy on us.*
God, the Son, Redeemer of the world,
have mercy on us.
God, the Holy Spirit, *have mercy on us.*
Holy Trinity, one God, *have mercy on us.*
Holy Mary, *pray for us* (repeat after each invocation).

Holy Mother of God,
Holy Virgin of virgins,
Mother of Christ,
Mother of the Church,
Mother of divine grace,
Mother most pure,
Mother most chaste,
Mother inviolate,
Mother undefiled,
Mother most amiable,
Mother most admirable,
Mother of good counsel,
Mother of our Creator,
Mother of our Savior,
Virgin most prudent,
Virgin most venerable,
Virgin most renowned,
Virgin most powerful,
Virgin most merciful,
Virgin most faithful,
Mirror of justice,
Seat of wisdom,
Cause of our joy,
Spiritual vessel,
Vessel of honor,
Singular vessel of devotion,
Mystical rose,
Tower of David,
Tower of ivory,
House of gold,
Ark of the Covenant,
Gate of heaven,
Morning star,
Health of the sick,
Refuge of sinners,

Comforter of the afflicted,
Help of Christians,
Queen of angels,
Queen of patriarchs,
Queen of prophets,
Queen of apostles,
Queen of martyrs,
Queen of confessors,
Queen of virgins,
Queen of all saints,
Queen conceived without original sin,
Queen assumed into heaven,
Queen of the most holy rosary,
Queen of families,
Queen of peace,
Lamb of God, who take away the sins of the world,
spare us, O Lord.
Lamb of God, who take away the sins of the world,
graciously hear us, O Lord.
Lamb of God, who take away the sins of the world,
have mercy on us.
Pray for us, O holy Mother of God,
that we may be made worthy of the promises of Christ.

Let us pray: Grant, we beseech You, O Lord God, that we Your servants may enjoy perpetual health of mind and body and, by the glorious intercession of the blessed Mary, ever virgin, be delivered from present sorrow, and obtain eternal joy. Through Christ our Lord. Amen.

We fly to your patronage, O holy Mother of God. Despise not our petitions in our necessities, but deliver us always from all dangers, O glorious and blessed Virgin. Amen.

8. **Prayer to St. Joseph.** St. Joseph, guardian of Jesus and

chaste spouse of Mary, you passed your life in perfect fulfillment of duty. You supported the Holy Family of Nazareth with the work of your hands. Kindly protect those who trustingly turn to you. You know their aspirations, their hardships, their hopes; and they turn to you because they know you will understand and protect them. You too have known trial, labor, and weariness. But, even amid the worries of material life, your soul was filled with deep peace and sang out in true joy through intimacy with the Son of God entrusted to you, and with Mary, His tender Mother. Amen.

— *(Pope John XXIII)*

9. **Litany of the Sacred Heart, promises of the Sacred Heart.**

Lord, have mercy on us.
Christ, have mercy on us.
Lord, have mercy on us. Christ, hear us.
Christ, graciously hear us.
God the Father of heaven,
have mercy on us (repeat after each invocation).
God the Son, Redeemer of the world,
God the Holy Spirit,
Holy Trinity, one God,
Heart of Jesus, Son of the eternal Father,
Heart of Jesus, formed by the Holy Spirit in the womb of the Virgin Mother,
Heart of Jesus, substantially united to the Word of God,
Heart of Jesus, of infinite majesty,
Heart of Jesus, sacred temple of God,
Heart of Jesus, tabernacle of the Most High,
Heart of Jesus, house of God and gate of heaven,
Heart of Jesus, burning furnace of charity,
Heart of Jesus, abode of justice and love,
Heart of Jesus, full of goodness and love,
Heart of Jesus, abyss of all virtues,

Heart of Jesus, most worthy of all praise,
Heart of Jesus, king and center of all hearts,
Heart of Jesus, in whom are all the treasures of wisdom and knowledge,
Heart of Jesus, in whom dwells the fullness of divinity,
Heart of Jesus, in whom the Father is well pleased,
Heart of Jesus, of whose fullness we have all received,
Heart of Jesus, desire of the everlasting hills,
Heart of Jesus, patient and most merciful,
Heart of Jesus, enriching all who invoke You,
Heart of Jesus, fountain of life and holiness,
Heart of Jesus, propitiation for our sins,
Heart of Jesus, loaded down with opprobrium,
Heart of Jesus, bruised for our offenses,
Heart of Jesus, obedient even to death,
Heart of Jesus, pierced with a lance,
Heart of Jesus, source of all consolation,
Heart of Jesus, our life and reconciliation,
Heart of Jesus, victim of sin,
Heart of Jesus, salvation of those who hope in You,
Heart of Jesus, hope of those who die in You,
Heart of Jesus, delight of all the saints,
Lamb of God, Who take away the sins of the world, *spare us, O Lord.*
Lamb of God, Who take away the sins of the world, *graciously hear us, O Lord.*
Lamb of God, Who take away the sins of the world, *have mercy on us.*
Jesus, meek and humble of heart, *make our hearts like unto Yours.*

Let us pray: O almighty and eternal God, look upon the Heart of Your dearly beloved Son and upon the praise and satisfaction He offers You in behalf of sinners and, being appeased, grant pardon to those who seek Your mercy, in the name of the same Jesus Christ, Your Son, Who lives and reigns with You, in the unity of the Holy Spirit, world without end. Amen.

Promises of Our Lord to those devoted to His Sacred Heart (these should be read by the prayer leader):

(1) I will give them all the graces necessary in their state of life.
(2) I will establish peace in their homes.
(3) I will comfort them in all their afflictions.
(4) I will be their refuge during life and above all in death.
(5) I will bestow a large blessing on all their undertakings.
(6) Sinners shall find in My Heart the source and the infinite ocean of mercy.
(7) Tepid souls shall grow fervent.
(8) Fervent souls shall quickly mount to high perfection.
(9) I will bless every place where a picture of My Heart shall be set up and honored.
(10) I will give to priests the gift of touching the most hardened hearts.
(11) Those who promote this devotion shall have their names written in My Heart, never to be blotted out.
(12) I promise you in the excessive mercy of My Heart that My all-powerful love will grant to all those who communicate on the first Friday in nine consecutive months the grace of final penitence; they shall not die in My disgrace nor without receiving their sacraments; My divine Heart shall be their safe refuge in this last moment.

10. **Prayer for Priests.** "Lord Jesus, Chief Shepherd of the Flock, we pray that in the great love and mercy of Your Sacred Heart You attend to all the needs of Your priest-shepherds throughout the world. We ask that You draw

back to Your Heart all those priests who have seriously strayed from Your path, that You rekindle the desire for holiness in the hearts of those priests who have become lukewarm, and that You continue to give Your fervent priests the desire for the highest holiness. United with Your Heart and Mary's Heart, we ask that You take this petition to Your heavenly Father in the unity of the Holy Spirit. Amen."

11. **Prayer for all members of the Shepherds of Christ Associates.** "Dear Jesus, we ask Your special blessings on all members of Shepherds of Christ Associates. Continue to enlighten them regarding the very special privilege and responsibility you have given them as members of Your movement, Shepherds of Christ Associates. Draw them ever closer to Your Heart and to Your Mother's Heart. Allow them to more and more realize the great and special love of Your Hearts for each of them as unique individuals. Give them the grace to respond to Your love and Mary's love with an increased love of their own. As they dwell in Your Heart and Mary's Heart, abundantly care for all their needs and those of their loved ones. We make our prayer through You to the Father, in the Holy Spirit, with Mary our Mother at our side. Amen."

12. **Prayer for the spiritual and financial success of the priestly newsletter.** "Father, we ask Your special blessings upon the priestly newsletter, Shepherds of Christ. We ask that You open the priest-readers to the graces You wish to give them through this chosen instrument of Your Son. We also ask that You provide for the financial needs of the newsletter and the Shepherds of Christ Associates. We make our prayer through Jesus, in the Holy Spirit, with Mary at our side. Amen."

13. **Prayer for all members of the human family.** "Heavenly Father, we ask Your blessings on all Your children the world over. Attend to all their needs. We ask Your special assistance for all those marginalized people, all those who are so neglected and forgotten. United with our Mother Mary, we make this petition to You through Jesus and in the Holy Spirit. Amen."

14. **Prayer to St. Michael and our Guardian Angels:** "St. Michael the Archangel, defend us in battle. Be our safeguard against the wickedness and snares of the devil. May God rebuke him, we humbly pray, and do thou, O prince of the heavenly hosts, by the power of God, cast into hell Satan and all the other evil spirits who prowl about the world seeking the ruin of souls. Amen."
"Angel of God, my guardian dear, to whom God's love commits me here, ever this day be at my side, to light and guard, to rule and guide. Amen."

15. **Pause for silent, personal prayer.** This should last at least five minutes.

16. **Act of consecration to the Sacred Heart of Jesus and the Immaculate Heart of Mary.**

    "Lord Jesus, Chief Shepherd of the flock, I consecrate myself to Your most Sacred Heart. From Your pierced Heart the Church was born, the Church You have called me, as a member of Shepherds of Christ Associates, to serve in a most special way. You reveal Your Heart as a symbol of Your love in all its aspects, including Your most special love for me, whom You have chosen as Your companion in this most important work. Help me to always love You in return. Help me to give myself entirely to You. Help me always to pour out my life in love of God and neighbor! Heart of Jesus, I place my trust in You!

"Dear Blessed Virgin Mary, I consecrate myself to your maternal and Immaculate Heart, this Heart which is symbol of your life of love. You are the Mother of my Savior. You are also my Mother. You love me with a most special love as a member of Shepherds of Christ Associates, a movement created by your Son as a powerful instrument for the renewal of the Church and the world. In a return of love, I give myself entirely to your motherly love and protection. You followed Jesus perfectly. You are His first and perfect disciple. Teach me to imitate you in the putting on of Christ. Be my motherly intercessor so that, through your Immaculate Heart, I may be guided to an ever closer union with the pierced Heart of Jesus, Chief Shepherd of the flock."

17. **Daily Prayers.** All members should say the Holy Spirit prayer daily and make the act of consecration daily. They should also pray the rosary each day. They are encouraged to use the other above prayers as time allows.

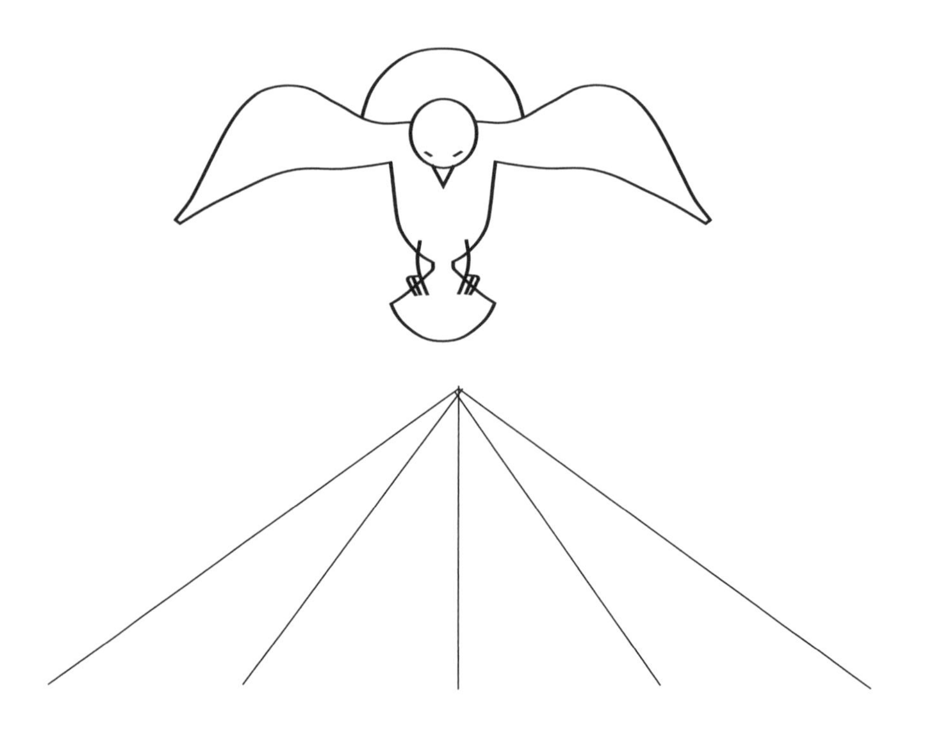

HOLY SPIRIT NOVENA

Shepherds of Christ Publications
Madison, Indiana

This book is published by Shepherds of Christ Publications, a subsidiary of Shepherds of Christ Ministries, a tax exempt religious public charitable association organized to foster devotion to the Two Hearts, the Sacred Heart of Jesus and the Immaculate Heart of Mary.

For additional copies, contact us:

Shepherds of Christ Ministries
P.O. Box 627
China, Indiana 47250 USA

(toll free number) 1-888-211-3041

(phone) 1-812-273-8405

(fax) 1-812-273-3182

http://www.SofC.org

Nihil Obstat:
Rev. Daniel J. Mahan, S.T.L.
Censor Librorum
Archdiocese of Indianapolis

Imprimatur:
Archbishop Daniel M. Buechlein, O.S.B.
Archbishop of Indianapolis
Archdiocese of Indianapolis

First Printing: March, 1999
Second Printing: April, 2000

DAILY NOVENA PRAYERS

Opening Prayer

In the name of the Father and of the Son and of the Holy Spirit. Amen.

Dear Father, we come to You in the name of Jesus, in union with Him in the Holy Sacrifice of the Mass, in the Holy Spirit. We come to You united to the Child Jesus of Good Health and the Infant of Prague. We come to You in the perfect, sinless heart of Our Mother Mary, asking her powerful intercession, uniting ourselves to her holy tears. We come to You united to all the angels and saints, and the souls in purgatory.

Prayer for Holy Spirit

We pray for an outpouring of the Holy Spirit on us, to be baptized by the Holy Spirit, that He will descend mightily on us as He did on the Apostles at Pentecost. That the Holy Spirit will transform us from fear to fearlessness and that He will give us courage to do all the Father is asking of us to help bring about the Reign of the Sacred Heart and the triumph of Mary's Immaculate Heart. We pray for the Holy Spirit to descend mightily on the Jesuits and the Poor Clares on the Shepherds of Christ leaders and members and on the whole Body of Christ and the world.

Protection by the Blood of Jesus

We pray that the Blood of Jesus will be spread on us, everyone in our families, and the Shepherds of Christ Movement, that we will be able to move steadfastly ahead and be protected from the evil one.

Healing

We pray for healing in body, mind, and soul and generational healing in ourselves, in all members in our families, and in all members of the Shepherds of Christ Movement, the Jesuit Community, the Poor Clares, the Body of Christ, and the world.

Prayer for Strength and Light

We adore You, oh Holy Spirit. Give us strength, give us light, console us. We give ourselves entirely to You. Oh Spirit of light and grace, we want to only do the will of the Father. Enlighten us that we may live always in the Father's will.

Eternal Spirit fill us with Your Divine Wisdom that we may

comprehend more fully insight into Your Divine Mysteries.

Give us lights, Oh Holy Spirit that we may know God. Work within the heart, the spiritual womb of the Virgin Mary, to form us more and more into the image of Jesus.

Prayer to Be One with God, Father, Son and Holy Spirit

We long for You, Oh Spirit of Light, we long to know God, we want to be one with Him, our Divine God. We want to be one with the Father, know Him as a Person most intimately. We want to know the beloved One, the Sacred Heart of Jesus, and live and dwell in Him at all times, every moment of our lives. We want to be one with You, Oh Spirit of Light, that You move in us in our every breath.

Prayer to Be One in Jesus

Let us experience life in the Sacred Heart of Jesus, so we can say as Saint Paul, "I have been crucified with Christ and yet I am alive; yet it is no longer I, but Christ living in me...." Let us live, united to the Mass, all through the day being one in Him. Let us be able to love and know in this elevated state of oneness with our God. We long for Thee, oh beauteous God, we love You, we love You, we love You. We praise You, worship You, honor You, adore You, and thank You, our beloved God, Father, Son, and Holy Spirit.

Prayer to Dwell in the Hearts of Jesus and Mary

We seek to be one in God, to live and dwell in the Hearts of Jesus and Mary, our little heaven on earth, to experience life in the all perfect, pure, sinless heart of our Mother. We want the Holy Spirit to move in us and to be united to Jesus as the Bridegroom of our souls and be a most perfect sacrifice offered to the Father at every moment as we unite in the Holy Sacrifice of the Mass around the world to help in the salvation of souls.

Prayer for the Holy Spirit and His Gifts

Come Holy Spirit, come, come into our hearts, inflame all people with the fire of Your love.

Leader: Send forth Your Spirit and all will be reborn.

All: And You will renew the face of the earth.

We pray for the seven gifts of the Holy Spirit, we ask for perfection in our souls to make us holy, holy souls likened to God.

Dear Holy Spirit, we give ourselves to You soul and body. We ask You to give us the Spirit of Wisdom, Understanding, Counsel, Fortitude, Knowledge, Piety, and Fear of the Lord.

Prayer for the Word Alive in Our Hearts

We know, dear Holy Spirit, the Word in His human nature was brought forth within the womb of the woman. We pray that His word will be brought forth in our hearts as He lives and dwells in us. We want the incarnation to go on in our lives. Dear Holy Spirit, work in us.

Little Prayers to the Holy Spirit

Dear Holy Spirit, help us not to be ignorant or indifferent or weak, help us to be strong with the love of God.

Dear Holy Spirit, please pray for our needs for us.

Dear Holy Spirit, help us to respect God and to avoid sin. Help us to live in the Father's will.

Dear Holy Spirit, help us to keep Your commandments and to respect authority. Help us to love all things as You will us to love them. Help us to want to pray and always serve God with the greatest love. Help us to know the truth. Help us to have the gift of faith, hope, and love. Help us to know what is right and what is wrong.

A Prayer for Intimacy with the Lamb, the Bridegroom of the Soul

Oh Lamb of God, Who take away the sins of the world, come and act on my soul most intimately. I surrender myself, as I ask for the grace to let go, to just be as I exist in You and You act most intimately on my soul. You are the Initiator. I am the soul waiting Your favors as You act in me. I love You. I adore You. I worship You. Come and possess my soul with Your Divine Grace, as I experience You most intimately.

FIRST WEEK MEDITATIONS NINE DAYS

1. **Romans 8:14-17**

   All who are guided by the Spirit of God are sons of God; for what you received was not the spirit of slavery to bring you back into fear; you received the Spirit of adoption, enabling us to cry out, 'Abba, Father!' The Spirit himself joins with our spirit to bear witness that we are children of God. And if we are children, then we are heirs, heirs of God and joint-heirs with Christ, provided that we share his suffering, so as to share his glory.

2. Romans 8:5-9

Those who are living by their natural inclinations have their minds on the things human nature desires; those who live in the Spirit have their minds on spiritual things. And human nature has nothing to look forward to but death, while the Spirit looks forward to life and peace, because the outlook of disordered human nature is opposed to God, since it does not submit to God's Law, and indeed it cannot, and those who live by their natural inclinations can never be pleasing to God. You, however, live not by your natural inclinations, but by the Spirit, since the Spirit of God has made a home in you. Indeed, anyone who does not have the Spirit of Christ does not belong to him.

3. 1 John 4:12-16

No one has ever seen God, but as long as we love one another God remains in us and his love comes to its perfection in us. This is the proof that we remain in him and he in us, that he has given us a share in his Spirit. We ourselves have seen and testify that the Father sent his Son as Saviour of the world. Anyone who acknowledges that Jesus is the Son of God, God remains in him and he in God. We have recognised for ourselves, and put our faith in, the love God has for us. God is love, and whoever remains in love remains in God and God in him.

4. 1 John 4:17-21

Love comes to its perfection in us when we can face the Day of Judgement fearlessly, because even in this world we have become as he is. In love there is no room for fear, but perfect love drives out fear, because fear implies punishment and no one who is afraid has come to perfection in love. Let us love, then, because he first loved us. Anyone who says 'I love God' and hates his brother, is a liar, since whoever does not love the brother whom he can see cannot love God whom he has not seen. Indeed this is the commandment we have received from him, that whoever loves God, must also love his brother.

5. 1 John 4:7-11

My dear friends, let us love one another, since love is from God and everyone who loves is a child of God and knows God. Whoever fails to love does not know God, because God is love. This is the revelation of God's love for us, that God sent his only Son into the world that we might have life through him. Love consists in this: it is not we who loved God, but God loved us and sent his Son to expiate our sins. My dear friends, if God loved us so much, we too should love one another.

6. Acts of the Apostles 1:1-5

In my earlier work, Theophilus, I dealt with everything Jesus had done and taught from the beginning until the day he gave his instructions to the apostles he had chosen through the Holy Spirit, and was taken up to heaven. He had shown himself alive to them after his Passion by many demonstrations: for forty days he had continued to appear to them and tell them about the kingdom of God. While at table with them, he had told them not to leave Jerusalem, but to wait there for what the Father had promised. 'It is', he had said, 'what you have heard me speak about: John baptised with water but, not many days from now, you are going to be baptised with the Holy Spirit.'

7. Acts of the Apostles 1:6-9

Now having met together, they asked him, 'Lord, has the time come for you to restore the kingdom to Israel?' He replied, 'It is not for you to know times or dates that the Father has decided by his own authority, but you will receive the power of the Holy Spirit which will come on you, and then you will be my witnesses not only in Jerusalem but throughout Judaea and Samaria, and indeed to earth's remotest end.'

As he said this he was lifted up while they looked on, and a cloud took him from their sight.

8. Acts of the Apostles 1:12-14

So from the Mount of Olives, as it is called, they went back to Jerusalem, a short distance away, no more than a Sabbath walk; and when they reached the city they went to the upper room where they were staying; there were Peter and John, James and Andrew, Philip and Thomas, Bartholomew and Matthew, James son of Alphaeus and Simon the Zealot, and Jude son of James. With one heart all these joined constantly in prayer, together with some women, including Mary the mother of Jesus, and with his brothers.

9. Acts of the Apostles 2:1-4

When Pentecost day came round, they had all met together, when suddenly there came from heaven a sound as of a violent wind which filled the entire house in which they were sitting; and there appeared to them tongues as of fire; these separated and came to rest on the head of each of them. They were all filled with the Holy Spirit and began to speak different languages as the Spirit gave them power to express themselves.

SECOND WEEK MEDITATIONS NINE DAYS

1. John 14:21-31

Whoever holds to my commandments and keeps them is the one who loves me; and whoever loves me will be loved by my Father, and I shall love him and reveal myself to him.'

Judas—not Judas Iscariot—said to him, 'Lord, what has happened, that you intend to show yourself to us and not to the world?' Jesus replied:

'Anyone who loves me will keep my word, and my Father will love him, and we shall come to him and make a home in him. Anyone who does not love me does not keep my words. And the word that you hear is not my own: it is the word of the Father who sent me. I have said these things to you while still with you; but the Paraclete, the Holy Spirit, whom the Father will send in my name, will teach you everything and remind you of all I have said to you. Peace I bequeath to you, my own peace I give you, a peace which the world cannot give, this is my gift to you. Do not let your hearts be troubled or afraid. You heard me say: I am going away and shall return. If you loved me you would be glad that I am going to the Father, for the Father is greater than I. I have told you this now, before it happens, so that when it does happen you may believe.

'I shall not talk to you much longer, because the prince of this world is on his way. He has no power over me, but the world must recognise that I love the Father and that I act just as the Father commanded. Come now, let us go.

2. John 17:11-26

I am no longer in the world, but they are in the world, and I am coming to you. Holy Father, keep those you have given me true to your name, so that they may be one like us. While I was with them, I kept those you had given me true to your name. I have watched over them and not one is lost except one who was destined to be lost, and this was to fulfil the scriptures. But now I am coming to you and I say these things in the world to share my joy with them to the full. I passed your word on to them, and the world hated them, because they belong to the world no more than I belong to the world. I am not asking you to remove them from the world, but to protect them from the Evil One. They do not belong to the world any more than I belong to the world. Consecrate them in the truth; your word is truth. As you sent me into the world, I have sent them into the world, and for their sake I consecrate myself so that they too may be consecrated in truth. I pray not only for these but also for those who through their teaching will come to believe in me. May they all be one, just as, Father, you are in me and I am in you, so that they also may be in us, so that the world may believe it was you who sent me. I have given them the glory you gave to me, that they may be one as we are one. With me in them and you in me, may they be so perfected in unity that the world will recognise that it was you who sent me and that you have loved them as you have loved me.

Father, I want those you have given me to be with me where I am, so that they may always see my glory which you have given me because you loved me before the foundation of the world. Father, Upright One, the world has not known you, but I have known you, and these have known that you have sent me. I have made your name known to them and will continue to make it known, so that the love with which you loved me may be in them, and so that I may be in them.

3. 1 Corinthians 15:20-28

In fact, however, Christ has been raised from the dead, as the first-fruits of all who have fallen asleep. As it was by one man that death came, so through one man has come the resurrection of the dead. Just as all die in Adam, so in Christ all will be brought to life; but all of them in their proper order: Christ the first-fruits, and next, at his coming, those who belong to him. After that will come the end, when he will hand over the kingdom to God the Father, having abolished every principality, every ruling force and power. For he is to be king until he has made his enemies his footstool, and the last of the enemies to be done away with is death, for he has put all things under his feet. But when it is said everything is subjected, this obviously cannot include the One who subjected everything to him. When everything has been subjected to him, then the Son himself will be subjected to the One who has subjected everything to him, so that God may be all in all.

4. Revelation 3:1-3,12,16-19

'Write to the angel of the church in Sardis and say, "Here is the message of the one who holds the seven spirits of God and the seven stars: I know about your behaviour: how you are reputed to be alive and yet are dead. Wake up; put some resolve into what little vigour you have left: it is dying fast. So far I have failed to notice anything in your behaviour that my God could possibly call perfect; remember how you first heard the message. Hold on to that. Repent! If you do not wake up, I shall come to you like a thief, and you will have no idea at what hour I shall come upon you.

Anyone who proves victorious I will make into a pillar in the sanctuary of my God, and it will stay there for ever; I will inscribe on it the name of my God and the name of the city of my God, the new Jerusalem which is coming down from my God in heaven, and my own new name as well.

'...but since you are neither hot nor cold, but only lukewarm, I will spit you out of my mouth. You say to yourself: I am rich, I have made a fortune and have everything I want, never realising that you are wretchedly and pitiably poor, and blind and naked too. I warn you, buy from me the gold that has been tested in the fire to make you truly rich, and white robes to clothe you and hide your shameful nakedness, and ointment to put on your eyes to enable you to see. I reprove and train those whom I love: so repent in real earnest.'

5. Revelation 5:9-14

They sang a new hymn: You are worthy to take the scroll and to break its seals, because you were sacrificed, and with your blood you bought people for God of every race, language, people and nation and made them a line of kings and priests for God, to rule the world.

In my vision, I heard the sound of an immense number of angels gathered round the throne and the living creatures and the elders; there were ten thousand times ten thousand of them and thousands upon thousands, loudly chanting:

Worthy is the Lamb that was sacrificed to receive power, riches, wisdom, strength, honour, glory and blessing. Then I heard all the living things in creation—everything that lives in heaven, and on earth, and under the earth, and in the sea, crying:

To the One seated on the throne and to the Lamb, be all praise, honour, glory and power, for ever and ever.

And the four living creatures said, 'Amen'; and the elders prostrated themselves to worship.

6. Revelation 7:14-17

I answered him, 'You can tell me, sir.' Then he said, 'These are the people who have been through the great trial; they have washed their robes white again in the blood of the Lamb. That is why they are standing in front of God's throne and serving him day and night in his sanctuary; and the One who sits on the throne will spread his tent over them. They will never hunger or thirst again; sun and scorching wind will never plague them, because the Lamb who is at the heart of the throne will be their shepherd and will guide them to springs of living water; and God will wipe away all tears from their eyes.'

7. Revelation 12:1-8

Now a great sign appeared in heaven: a woman, robed with the sun, standing on the moon, and on her head a crown of twelve stars. She was pregnant, and in labour, crying aloud in the pangs of childbirth. Then a second sign appeared in the sky: there was a huge red dragon with seven heads and ten horns, and each of the seven heads crowned with a coronet. Its tail swept a third of the stars from the sky and hurled them to the ground, and the dragon stopped in front of the woman as she was at the point of giving birth, so that it could eat the child as soon as it was born. The woman was delivered of a boy, the son who was to rule all the nations with an iron sceptre, and the child was taken straight up to God and to his throne, while the woman escaped into the desert, where God had prepared a place for her to be looked after for twelve hundred and sixty days.

And now war broke out in heaven, when Michael with his angels attacked the dragon. The dragon fought back with his angels, but they were defeated and driven out of heaven.

8. Revelation 14:1-7

Next in my vision I saw Mount Zion, and standing on it the Lamb who had with him a hundred and forty-four thousand people, all with his name and his Father's name written on their foreheads. I heard a sound coming out of heaven like the sound of the ocean or the roar of thunder; it was like the sound of harpists playing their harps. There before the throne they were singing a new hymn in the presence of the four living creatures and the elders, a hymn that could be learnt only by the hundred and forty-four thousand who had been redeemed from the world. These are the sons who have kept their virginity and not been defiled with women; they follow the Lamb wherever he goes; they, out of all people, have been redeemed to be the first-fruits for God and for the Lamb. No lie was found in their mouths and no fault can be found in them.

Then I saw another angel, flying high overhead, sent to announce the gospel of eternity to all who live on the earth, every nation, race, language and tribe. He was calling, 'Fear God and glorify him, because the time has come for him to sit in judgement; worship the maker of heaven and earth and sea and the springs of water.'

Revelation 19: 7-8

let us be glad and joyful and give glory to God, because this is the time for the marriage of the Lamb. His bride is ready, and she has been able to dress herself in dazzling white linen, because her linen is made of the good deeds of the saints.'

9. Revelation 21:1-10

Then I saw a new heaven and a new earth; the first heaven and the first earth had disappeared now, and there was no longer any sea. I saw the holy city, the new Jerusalem, coming down out of heaven from God, prepared as a bride dressed for her husband. Then I heard a loud voice call from the throne, 'Look, here God lives among human beings. He will make his home among them; they will be his people, and he will be their God, God-with-them. He will wipe away all tears from their eyes; there will be no more death, and no more mourning or sadness or pain. The world of the past has gone.'

Then the One sitting on the throne spoke. 'Look, I am making the whole of creation new. Write this, "What I am saying is trustworthy and will come true." ' Then he said to me, 'It has already happened. I am the Alpha and the Omega, the Beginning and the End. I will give water from the well of life free to anybody who is thirsty; anyone who proves victorious will inherit these things; and I will be his God and he will be my son. But the legacy for cowards, for those who break their word, or worship obscenities, for murderers and the sexually immoral, and for sorcerers, worshippers of false gods or any other sort of liars, is the second death in the burning lake of sulphur.'

One of the seven angels that had the seven bowls full of the seven final plagues came to speak to me and said, 'Come here and I will show you the bride that the Lamb has married.' In the spirit, he carried me to the top of a very high mountain, and showed me Jerusalem, the holy city, coming down out of heaven from God.

Revelation 22:20

The one who attests these things says: I am indeed coming soon.

Amen; come, Lord Jesus.

Other great books published by Shepherds of Christ Publications

To order any of the following materials please contact us by mail, phone, fax, email or the Internet:

Shepherds of Christ Publications
P.O. Box 627
China, Indiana 47250 USA

Toll free USA: (888) 211-3041
Tel: (812) 273-8405 Fax: (812) 273-3182
Email: info@sofc.org http://www.sofc.org

Please contact us for *Prayer Manuals* or to begin a Prayer Chapter to pray for the priests, the Church and the world.

C1.	*The Word Alive in Our Hearts - Partial Cycle A*	$5
C2.	*Focusing on the Word - Complete Cycle B*	$15
C3.	*Feed My Soul - Complete Cycle C*	$15
C4.	*Steadfast to the Son - Complete Cycle A*	$15
C5.	*Reflect on the Word - Complete Cycle B (this book)*	$15

Guiding Light homily series by the Reverend Joe Robinson given at St. Boniface Church in Cincinnati, Ohio. It is a tremendous honor Fr. Joe has allowed us to share these great gifts with you – for greater holiness and knowing more and more about God.

B8. *Mass Book*, by Rita Ring: Many of the entries in the Priestly Newsletter Volume II from a spiritual journal came from this book. These entries are to help people to be more deeply united to God in the Mass. This book is available in English and Spanish with the Church's *Imprimatur*. $12

BN4. *Response to God's Love* by Fr. Edward J. Carter, S.J. In this book Fr. Carter speaks of God as the ultimate mystery. We can meditate on the interior life of the Trinity. Fr. Carter tells us about our uniqueness in the Father's Plan for us, how the individual Christian, the Church and the world are in the state of becoming. *Imprimatur*. $10

BN3. *Shepherds of Christ - Volume 3* by Fr. Edward J. Carter, S.J. Contains Newsletter Issues 1 through 4 of 2000 including Fr. Carter's tremendous *Overview of the Spiritual Life* $10

BN2. *Shepherds of Christ - Volume 2*: by Fr. Edward J. Carter, S.J. Contains issues 13-29 of the newsletter (September/October 1996 - Issue 5, 1999) $15

BN1. *Shepherds of Christ - Selected Writings on Spirituality for all People* as Published in Shepherds of Christ Newsletter for Priests. Contains 12 issues of the newsletter from July/August 1994 to May/June 1996. $15

B7. *Rosary Meditations for Parents and Children*, by Rita Ring, Short Meditations for both parents and children to be used when praying the rosary. These meditations will help all to know the lives of Jesus and Mary alive in their Hearts. Available in both English and Spanish with the Church's *Imprimatur*. $10

Shepherds of Christ Ministries

Send Order To:
Shepherds of Christ Ministries
P.O. Box 627
China, Indiana 47250 USA

Order Form

	Qty	Total $
P1. Prayer Manuals	____	______
C1. The Word Alive in Our Hearts ($5)	____	______
C2. Focusing on the Word - Cycle B ($15)	____	______
C3. Feed My Soul - Cycle C ($15)	____	______
C4. Guiding Light - Cycle A ($15)	____	______
C5. Reflect on the Word - Cycle B ($15)	____	______
B8. Mass Book ($12)	____	______
BN4. Response to God's Love ($10)	____	______
BN3. Shepherds of Christ - Volume 3 ($10)	____	______
BN2. Shepherds of Christ - Volume 2 ($15)	____	______
BN1. Shepherds of Christ - Volume 1 ($15)	____	______
B7. Rosary Meditations for Parents and Children ($10)	____	______
Totals:	____	______

Name: ______________________________________

Address: ____________________________________

City: ______________ State: __________ Zip: _________

For More Information Call Toll free USA: 1-888-211-3041
or on the Internet: www.sofc.org

Building the Kingdom of Truth

The Eucharist and the Word is the Bread of Life – In this world with distorted vision – we spread this book to you – Focusing on the Word – The Word alive in our Hearts – Reflecting on the Word – THIS IS TRUTH

The more we live the Word in our lives, the more we live Jesus' life, death, and resurrection in our lives – the more we know the truth and see more clearly the vision of our heavenly Father –

We have been given the Catholic Church – Pillar of truth – We have been given the Word – We have been given the Commandments –

Because of original sin we have distorted vision – Living in the Word . . obeying the Commandments – Living according to the Church's teachings helps us to live in the truth – to see more the vision of the Father – We know in this distorted world – THE TRUTH! !

We pray the Our Father at Mass – We focus on our Heavenly Father and His Plan for us – We want unity as children of God

In spreading these homilies and our writings on the Eucharist – we want men to be fed more and more with the Bread of Life – We want to live in the truth – We want to live in greater faith, hope and love – To live in unity –

To date – 17 years – we have circulated 15,000,000 Priestly Newsletters loose and in books from Fr. Carter and other priests.

We have begun prayer chapters in 8 languages with the Church's Imprimatur, around the world, so there is a network of prayer out there praying for our priests, the Church and the world –

If we have this devotion to the Sacred Heart and Immaculate Heart, we are helping ourselves to be more united in the pure and holy Hearts of Jesus and Mary as Mary asked for at Fatima –

When we die there will be a network of prayer around the world praying for our beloved priests and the Church –

This to me is the greatest gift I can give to my children and grandchildren in helping more and more our holy priests – We hope people love God and others as they dwell in the Hearts of Jesus and Mary.

We pray people love the Church more and more and thank God for this precious gift of the Church and the priest and the Word – We pray people live as strong members of the mystical body of Christ –

The world is in so much need of prayer and that deep relationship with Mary, Mother of the Church – The Holy Spirit works in that Spousal union with Mary helping us to do God's will –

Thank you for your willingness to answer God's call in focusing on the Word and praying for the priests, the Church and the world with us –

May God bless you in your mission of loving and serving God and helping to build the Kingdom of God.

May the Light of Christ shine on the earth as we live more holy lives in Him and in His Word –

We should respond enthusiastically to Christ's call to help build up the Kingdom of truth and love, of justice and that the peace of Christ is spread on this earth.

The Shepherds of Christ Movement

Co-equal purpose

Ministries

1. **PRIMARY MINISTRY** - CIRCULATING PRIESTLY NEWSLETTERS TO PRIESTS ALL OVER THE WORLD IN ENGLISH AND SPANISH to promote priestly holiness, Fr. Joe's books and other priests books –

2. **PRAYER CHAPTERS** praying for the priests and the renewal of the Church and the world using the prayer manual (in 8 languages with the Church's Imprimatur).

3. School Rosary Program and Junior Shepherds of Christ Ministry.
4. Nursing Home Ministry.
5. Special retreats and adoration before the Blessed Sacrament.
6. Apostles of the Eucharistic Heart of Jesus.
7. Promoting the rosary to all, rosary meditations.
8. Prison Ministry to promote prayer and spiritual renewal.
9. Handmaids and Servants of the Good Shepherd.
10. Audio/Video Departments (priestly newsletters on tape).
11. Prayer books, newsletters, newsletter books, and other spiritual aids.

John 15: 5-6

I am the vine, you are the branches. Whoever remains in me, with me in him, bears fruit in plenty; for cut off from me you can do nothing. Anyone who does not remain in me is thrown away like a branch –and withers; these branches are collected and thrown on the fire and are burnt.

We get our life from Jesus – He is the vine – we are the branches – A branch cannot bear grapes if it is disconnected from the vine – We cannot do anything without Him

Sing: Bread of Life

John 17: 21

May they all be one, …

We want to follow Christ! We are to witness to Christ! We are to live in the truth!

Oh God send laborers into the harvest — Send those who will help us spread the Good News. Send us so many young and eager priests wanting to serve You —

by Rita Robinson Ring, Cofounder